What

DIFFICULTIES

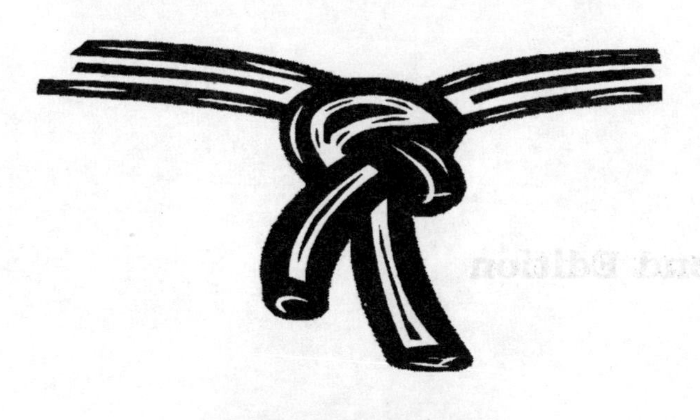

STRIKE

Published by:
Gita Publishing House
Sadhu Vaswani Mission,
10, Sadhu Vaswani Path,
Pune -411 001, (India).
gph@sadhuvaswani.org

Second Edition

ISBN : 978-93-80743-44-8

Printed by:
Mehta Offset Pvt. Ltd.
Mehta House,
A-16, Naraina Industrial Area II,
New Delhi-110 028, (India).
info@mehtaoffset.com

What to Do When DIFFICULTIES

STRIKE

J.P. VASWANI

GITA PUBLISHING HOUSE
PUNE, (INDIA).
www.dadavaswanisbooks.org

Other Books and Booklets by Dada J.P. Vaswani

In English:
10 Commandments of A Successful Marriage
108 Pearls of Practical Wisdom
108 Simple Prayers of A Simple Man
108 Thoughts on Success
114 Thoughts on Love
A Little Book of Life
A Simple And Easy Way To God
A Treasure of Quotes
Around The Camp Fire
Begin The Day With God
Bhagavad Gita in a Nutshell
Burn Anger Before Anger Burns You
Daily Inspiration
Daily Inspiration (Booklet)
Destination Happiness
Dewdrops of Love
Does God Have Favourites?
Ecstasy and Experiences
Formula For Prosperity
Gateways to Heaven
God In Quest of Man
Good Parenting
Gurukul
Gurukul II
How To Overcome Depression
I am a Sindhi
In 2012 All Will Be Well
Joy Peace Pills
Kill Fear Before Fear Kills You
Ladder of Abhyasa
Lessons Life Has Taught Me
Life After Death
Management Moment by Moment
Mantras For Peace Of Mind
Many Paths: One Goal
Nearer, My God, To Thee!
New Education Can Make the World New
Peace or Perish
Positive Power of Thanksgiving
Questions Answered
Sadhu Vaswani : His Life And Teachings
Saints For You and Me
Saints With A Difference
Secrets of Health And Happiness
Shake Hand With Life
Short Sketches of Saints Known & Unknown
Sketches of Saints Known & Unknown
Stop Complaining: Start Thanking!
Swallow Irritation Before Irritation Swallows You
Teachers are Sculptors
The Goal Of Life and How To Attain It
The Little Book of Freedom From Stress
The Little Book of Prayer
The Little Book of Service
The Little Book of Success
The Little Book of Wisdom
The Little Book of Yoga
The Magic of Forgiveness
The Perfect Relationship: Guru and Disciple
The Seven Commandments of the Bhagavad Gita
The Terror Within
The Way of Abhyasa (How To Meditate)
Thus Have I Been Taught
Tips For Teenagers
What You Would Like To know About Karma
What You Would Like To know About Hinduism
Why Do Good People Suffer?
You Are Not Alone God Is With You!

Story Books:
101 Stories For You And Me
25 Stories For Children and also for Teens
It's All A Matter of Attitude
Snacks For The Soul
More Snacks For The Soul
Break The Habit
The Lord Provides
The Heart of a Mother
The King of Kings
The One Thing Needful
The Patience of Purna
The Power of Good Deeds
The Power of Thought
Trust Me All in All or Not at All
Whom Do You Love the Most
You Can Make A Difference

In Hindi:
Aalwar Santon Ki Mahan Gaathaayen
Atmik Jalpaan
Aapkay Karm, Aapkaa Bhaagy Banaatay Hein
Atmik Poshan
Bhakton Ki Uljhanon Kaa Saral Upaai
Bhale Logon Ke Saath Bura Kyon?
Dainik Prerna
Dar Se Mukti Paayen
Ishwar Tujhe Pranam
Jiski Jholi Mein Hain Pyaar
Krodh Ko Jalayen Swayam Ko Nahin
Laghu Kathayein
Mrutyu Hai Dwar... Phir Kya?
Nava Pushp (Bhajans In Hindi and Sindhi)
Prarthna ki Shakti
Pyar Ka Masiha
Sadhu Vaswani: Unkaa Jeevan Aur Shikshaayen
Safal Vivah Ke Dus Rahasya
Santon Ki Leela
Sri Bhagavad Gita: Gaagar Mein Saagar

In Marathi:
Krodhala Shaanth Kara, Krodhane Ghala Ghalnya Purvee (Burn Anger Before Anger Burns You)
Jiski Jholi Mein Hain Pyaar
Life After Death
Pilgrim of Love
Sind and the Sindhis
Sufi Sant (Sufi Saints of East and West)
What You Would Like To Know About Karma

Other Publications:

Recipe Books:
90 Vegetarian Sindhi Recipes
Di-li-cious Vegetarian Recipes
Simply Vegetarian

Books on Dada J. P. Vaswani:
A Pilgrim of Love
Dada J.P. Vaswani: His Life and Teachings
Dada J.P. Vaswani's Historic Visit to Sind
Dost Thou Keep Memory
How To Embrace Pain
Living Legend
Moments with a Master

Contents

Chapter 1

THE GIFT OF FAITH

When I address Youth Meets or have a Question-Answer session with students, I am often asked this question: what is the one gift that you would ask of God if He were to appear before you and grant you a single boon?

Never mind what I would ask: if such a happy event were to befall you, I would strongly urge you to ask God for the great gift of faith!

Faith is the spirit that sustains life. Faith is the ray of sunshine that lights up the dark, deep caverns of the human heart. Faith is the elixir of the soul. Faith is the beautiful, fragrant flower that blooms even in the wilderness of despair and suffering. Faith is the one true source of support on which we can always rely in the rough and tough journey called life upon this earth. Faith is the sustenance for all human endeavours. It is the greatest blessing that God can bestow upon us!

A man may be affluent and possess enough material wealth to leave to successive future generations of his family; he may be in the enjoyment of "the boast of heraldry, the pomp of power," as the poet puts it. But, let me tell you, if he lacks faith, his wealth and power are as nothing; indeed he is no better than a man afflicted with utter poverty – poverty of the spirit! On the other hand, a man may not possess much, he may be poor in the wealth of this world, but if he has faith in God, then he is indeed a fortunate soul, who lacks nothing. A man of faith, I know, lives in stability and equanimity.

May I give you the inspiring words of Gurudev Sadhu Vaswani:

> Faith wins!
> Believe, and the world's opposition will wither, as withered the fig tree at Jesus's word!
> Faith wins!

If you have not heard of the episode of the fig-tree from the New Testament, let me narrate it to you. It is said that one day, early in the morning, as he was on his way to a city, Jesus became hungry. Seeing a fig tree by the road, he went up to it but found nothing on it except leaves. Then he said to it, "May you never bear fruit again!" Immediately the tree withered.

When the disciples saw this, they were amazed. "How did the fig tree wither so quickly?" they asked.

Jesus replied, "I tell you the truth, if you have faith and do not doubt, not only can you do what was done to the fig tree, but also you can say to this mountain,

'Go, throw yourself into the sea,' and it will be done. If you believe, you will receive whatever you ask for in prayer."

Christian scholars explain this incident by saying that it teaches us the principle that religious "profession" and observançes are not enough to guarantee salvation, unless there is the fruit of genuine salvation evident in the life of the person. As the Apostle James would put it later: "Faith without works is dead". (James 2:26)

Sri Ramakrishna expresses the concept of faith with his characteristic simplicity which is actually profundity of the highest order:

> Unless one has the faith of a baby, one cannot have access to the Lord. If the mother points to someone and says, "He is your father," the baby believes it. The grace of the Lord comes to Him who has this kind of faith. The calculating and the doubtful estrange themselves from the Divine.

Rishis of our ancient India, time and again offered the immortal prayer, "*Tamso Maa Jyotir Gamaya.*" "O Lord, lead me out of darkness into Light." This light is the light of faith; this illumination which dispels the darkness is faith. The illumination has one message, "God, You are my protector, You are with me, You are watching me, You are watching over me." This faith of God's constant presence with him, illumines the soul of man.

Shraddhaavaan labhate jnaanam...

The man of faith obtains wisdom: so the Lord tells us in the Bhagavad Gita. The essential thing is faith: for all else will follow. But he who has no faith, who is of a doubting nature, goes to destruction, the Lord warns His dear, devoted disciple, Arjuna. For the doubting self, there is neither this world, nor that beyond, nor happiness.

Ch IV – 40.

What is faith? Faith is not blind, as some 'rationalists' would claim. Faith is *seeing* with the eyes of the heart. But alas, with many of us, the eyes of the heart are closed. When we open these eyes, we will see that all that has happened has happened for the best, all that is happening is happening for the best, and all that will happen will happen for the best. There is a meaning of mercy in all that happens. God has a plan for everyone of us, and there is divine purpose in every little thing that happens to us. As the great American poet, Whittier, put it, "When faith is lost...the man is dead!"

Etymologists tell us that the English word faith is derived from the Latin root *fidem,* or *fides*, meaning trust. There is a beautiful Eighteenth century sculpture, called "The allegory of faith", which represents a veiled countenance, with eyes closed. The veil signifies man's impossibility to know the concrete 'evidence' which is required by rationalists and logicians! On one end of the spectrum of belief is what scholars call 'logical positivism', which insists on the concrete evidence of the senses, and therefore denies the validity of all beliefs held by faith; on the other extreme is 'fideism', which holds that true belief can only arise from faith, because reason and evidence alone, can never lead us to the truth.

Let me give you the words of Blaise Pascal: "Faith certainly tells us what the senses do not, but not the contrary of what they see; it is above, not against them." Or, as a believer puts it, "Faith is not belief without proof, but trust without reservation."

This reminds me of the philosopher Will Durant, whose brilliant history of civilisation, tells us that The Age of faith was long ago superceded by the Age of reason.

If this be true, it is indeed a pity! For, in the words of Gurudev Rabindranath Tagore, "Faith is the bird that sings when the dawn is still dark."

May I tell you, faith is not blind! Faith is seeing with the eyes of the mind. Even as we have two physical eyes with which we see the wonderful world around us – trees, flowers, streams, hills, dales, forests, stars and sky – even so, with the eyes of faith we can perceive goodness, peace and joy all around us.

It has been said that faith sees the invisible, believes the incredible and receives the impossible. When fear knocks on the door of your heart, send faith to open it and you will be free from distress.

Faith is believing that God loves each and every one of us. He has a plan for us. He will provide for all our needs. Faith is seeking refuge in the Lord, trusting Him fully, completely, entirely. For His is the One Light that shines, shines and ever shines! Though the storms howl and the darkness grows deeper, His Light will continue to shine on us! He is nearer to us than our heartbeats and closer than our breathing. He is the All Powerful One whose hands are everywhere. He is all we need as a friend, as a helper, a guide, guardian and protector. There is not a corner too remote for His help to reach us. He is the All-loving One whose ears are ever attentive to the prayers of His wayward children. He is the All-knowing One who will do the very best for us. With Him all things are possible; and if He chooses not to do certain things which we want him to do, let us realise – it is not because He cannot do them, but because He knows that they are not for our good.

The one lesson we all need to learn is – utter dependence upon God. Everything else will follow. In the words of Kahlil Gibran, "Faith is a knowledge within the heart, beyond the reach of proof."

I am sure my readers know that in common parlance, we equate the term 'religion' with 'faith'. Thus, we talk of the Hindu faith. It would be no exaggeration to say that faith is the foundation of all religious belief; faith in God, faith in His Omnipotence, Omnipresence and Omniscience; faith in the scriptures; faith in the utterances of the Holy Ones. When faith is firm, I would say it has the power to transcend reason, without actually going against reason! Let us not forget: Faith also means confidence, belief, loyalty or allegiance. The Sanskrit equivalent is *shraddha.*

I am sure that all of you have heard and indeed, been inspired by this incident from the childhood of Sant Nam Dev. It is the custom of pious Mahrashtrian women, even now, to offer the food cooked by them as *naivedya* to the Lord in any nearby temple, before the family partakes of the food. Nam Dev's mother Guna Bai too had this habit. She would take a plate of freshly cooked food to the temple at Pandharpur, to offer to God Vitthal, before the family sat down to eat lunch. Thus, every meal was eaten as *prasad* in their devout family. One day, Guna Bai was unable to go to the temple herself; so she asked her young son, Nam Dev to take the food to the temple and offer it to the Lord.

The young boy happily agreed to do so, and set off for the temple. He set the plate before the Deity, closed his eyes tightly and begged the Lord to accept the food he had brought. But to his dismay, when he opened his eyes, he found the food on the plate untouched. For him, *naivedya* was not just a show-and-take-away ritual. He closed his eyes once again, and implored the Lord to accept the food. When the food was still left untouched, the boy began to shed bitter tears. "Vitthala! Vitthala!" he called out piteously, "Don't you like me? Are you angry with me, that you refuse to touch the food I have brought to you?"

Lord Vitthoba, as we know, is tender-hearted! He could not bear the grief of His dear devotee. So he appeared in human form and promptly ate the food placed before him! Seeing the empty plate, Nam Dev was happy, and returned home to inform his mother that the food had indeed been offered to God.

To say that Guna Bai was mystified by the empty plate would be an understatement. But she was a woman who never spoke in haste. She did not trouble her young son with the how and why and wherefore of the incident as some mothers still do! But the following day, she entrusted her son with the same errand; and she secretly followed him to the temple to see what he did with the food. To her amazement, she saw Nama close his eyes and pray to Vitthala; and she saw the Lord appear in human form and eat the food placed before Him!

"To one who has faith, no explanation is necessary. To one without faith, no explanation is possible," said St. Thomas of Aquinas.

The life of man is powered by faith. We repose our faith in our parents when we are young. As we grow older, friends, family, spouses, partners are added to the list of people we trust. We have faith in the law of the land, in the system of justice and governance; we have faith in democracy; we have faith in medicine and doctors. How can we survive without the faith that subsumes all these faiths? How can we survive without faith in God?

The Gift of Faith: A Recap for You:

1. May God grant us the gift of steadfast faith. It is the greatest blessing that God can bestow upon us!
2. The incident of Jesus Christ and the fig tree teaches the principle that without faith, mere religious profession and observance cannot guarantee salvation.
3. Faith is not blind. It 'sees' with the eyes of the heart.
4. There is a divine purpose in every little thing that happens to us. True belief can only arise from faith.
5. Faith is believing that God loves you. Therefore, let us cultivate faith in the Lord.
6. Kahlil Gibran- "Faith is Knowledge within the heart, beyond the reach of proof."
7. Faith is not Synonymous with religion, but is the foundation of all religious belief.
8. The relationship between Nam Dev and Lord Vittoba shows that faith does not actually go against reason; but, it does transcend reason.
9. Faith is an integral part of our lives. Form a close bond with God and repose your faith in Him.

Chapter 2

FAITH IS THE KEY!

"Optimism is nothing but the faith that leads to achievement. Nothing can be done without faith and hope and confidence."

The lady who spoke those words was one whose name is synonymous with faith and hope and optimism: she was none other than Helen Keller who overcame the severest disability to become a woman of achievement, a woman of substance!

We may not all be high achievers like Helen Keller; the glare of fame and adulation may not ever throw its spotlight on us; but the least of us, the most insignificant among us lives by faith.

What I mean by faith here is not doctrinal or sectarian faith. It is not the kind of faith that claims to be 'superior' to all other faiths. It is the spirit that makes of our ordinary, human life, an offering to the Divine, a pilgrimage to the Eternal. Faith is the *paras mani*, the philosopher's stone that transforms all life's *dukkha* (sorrows) into a triumph and a celebration.

Is this not the spirit in which devout Christians celebrate the birth of Jesus? For, the life of Jesus, or even the death of Jesus, was by no means a tragedy. It was a triumph for God and man. It was an event that reopened the gates of paradise for all mankind.

"... For whosoever believeth in Him should not perish, but have eternal life..."

Is not this kind of faith the key to a life of hope and fulfillment?

Life cannot pose a question which faith cannot answer; life cannot present a problem which fear cannot solve; life cannot expose you to a sorrow or suffering which faith cannot surmount.

Therefore, the great thinker and writer, Thomas Merton tells us:

> Faith is the only key to the Universe. The final meaning of human existence, and the answers to the questions on which all our happiness depends, cannot be found in any other way.

Let us be clear about one thing: faith is not the equivalent of an Alladin's lamp or an "Open sesame!" which will instantaneously produce before us, all that we desire. Nor does faith offer us the guarantee that we will never come face to face with sorrow, suffering, weakness or disappointment. But faith can give us the courage, the right attitude and the ability to face up to those problems and emerge victorious.

The Bible tells us: "If you have faith as a grain of a mustard seed... nothing shall be impossible unto you."

The Master who spoke these words knew human nature well! He knew that we are men and women 'of little faith'. Therefore, we are given the promise: "According to your faith be it given unto you."

It was the year 1910. Gurudev Sadhu Vaswani was in Europe. He had visited several places and addressed eager audiences on the message of India's Rishis and Saints. His address at the *Welt-Congress*, the World Congress of Religions at Berlin and his subsequent lectures in different parts of Europe aroused deep interest in Indian thought and religion, and awakened in many hearts love for God and the suffering children of God. When his work in Europe was over and he was ready to return to India, he found he did not have money to purchase a ticket. He did not worry: he knew that a ticket would be provided at the right time.

A day before the steamer was to set sail for India, he was invited by the Maharani of Cooch Behar to take tea with her. She was in England on a holiday trip. In the course of her talk, the Maharani said to Gurudev, "May I make a request?"

Sadhu Vaswani smiled.

The Maharani said, "I understand you have finished your work in Europe and are returning to India. Please permit me to get your ticket for you."

Sadhu Vaswani was not surprised. The life of a man whose faith reposes in the Lord, is filled with many such 'miracles'. They are not really miracles: they are normal, natural workings of the Divine Mother who anticipates the needs of Her trusting children and provides for them. Wondrous are her ways! Blessed be Her Name!

In a beautiful *sloka* in Bhagavad Gita, the Lord makes a tremendous promise. "If a man meditates on Me and Me alone, and worships Me always and everywhere," He says, "to him I supply whatever he does not possess and preserve whatever he already possesses."

Ignorant people dismiss faith as mere emotionalism. They regard faith as a persistent illusion in which weak and incapable people take refuge from reality.

Faith is not weak. Faith is not sentimentalism. And faith is not always easy!

Once, Mother Teresa was being interviewed for BBC Television. The interviewer remarked that in a way, the life of service might be much easier for her than for ordinary householders. After all, he pointed out, she had no possessions, no insurance, no car, and no husband to care for!

Mother Teresa smiled and said to him, "I'm married too!" She held up the ring that nuns of the Order of the Sisters of Charity wear, to symbolise their 'marriage' to Christ. She added, "He can be very difficult at times!"

Mother Teresa faced many difficulties and trials. Like many saints, she too, had to pass through 'The dark Night of the Soul' – a phase of pessimism and despair. But her faith survived against all odds; in fact, it also gave her a wonderful sense of humour. She once remarked to a friend: "I know God will not give me anything I can't handle. I just wish He didn't trust me so much."

It takes courage to cultivate faith!

Atheists and rationalists tend to simply disregard faith as the refuge of cowards. That is because they can never have the inner courage and the moral power that is required to attain to faith. In fact, according to the great *acharyas* of Hinduism, faith can be nurtured only through tremendous self-discipline and effort of the will. Swami Sivananda tells us that true faith is "intuitive realisation of God Almighty through intense love and affection for Him." According to him, we can achieve this by following the eleven fundamental factors which Sri Ramanuja had prescribed. They are:

1. *Abhyasa* or the practice of continuous thinking of God;
2. *Viveka* or discrimination;
3. *Vimoka* or freedom from everything else and longing for God;
4. *Satyam* or truthfulness;
5. *Arjavam* or straightforwardness;
6. *Kriya* or doing good to others;
7. *Kalyana* or wishing well-being to all;
8. *Daya* or compassion;
9. *Ahimsa* or non-injury;
10. *Dana* or charity;
11. *Anavasada* or cheerfulness and optimism.

Faith is not for the faint-hearted!

For those of you who are daunted by the list of *sadhanas,* let me offer a simplified version, the Little Way of cultivating faith the way of humble devotion, prescribed by Gurudev Sadhu Vaswani:

- by associating with people whose faith is strong.
- through daily self-analysis which always helps in building faith.
- by the daily practice of meditation.
- by a little of selfless service.
- through constant prayer.

God gives us many gifts, but if he takes away any one of them, we feel miserable and inconsolable. We begin to blame God. Why me? Why did this have to happen, we begin to question. Happiness belongs to those who are immersed in the faith, that God can never fail us. That the Great Universe has a perfect scheme of things and whatever happens, has a meaning and a purpose, which is good for us. We should accept the Divine Will as the *prasad* from God! Such an attitude can be cultivated by praying to God:

> Keep me close to your heart,
> Let me not wander,
> In joy and in sorrow,
> Thy Will, not mine, be done!

For those of us who live by our faith, as well as those who place their belief on 'science', life poses a series of unanswered – at times unanswerable questions. Why do bad things happen to good people? Why does a young, intelligent man, husband, father, brother and son to a family of wonderful people have to die of a rare, unheard form of cancer? Why are beautiful young babies sometimes born blind or deformed or spastic? Why are the nations of this world piling up a nuclear arsenal that can destroy the planet ten times over? Why is it that infections from cows, chickens and pigs turn out to be pandemics that create mass fear psychosis?

Truly it has been said, to be sentenced to life is to be sentenced to death! Therefore is it said, cowards die several deaths.

The Bhagavad Gita tells us:

> Meet the transient world
> With neither grasping nor fear,
> Trust the unfolding of life
> And you will attain true serenity.

Life is full of uncertainties, the unknown and the unknowable. Experts recommend that we develop what they call, "a high tolerance for uncertainty" if we are to live in peace, even while being aware that so much in our lives is *outside* our control. Losing control, living with uncertainty, generates stress and unhappiness – and this kind of trauma can be conquered by the right attitude – by faith and devotion.

Think about it...

Have you heard of *Guideposts*? It was started as a small four-page leaflet by the bestselling writer and preacher Norman Vicent Peale over sixty years ago; he edited and printed the leaflet from a small room on top of his garage at that time. Today it is one of the most popular testimonial magazines, selling over four million copies in the U.S. with a staff of more than six hundred people. A former editor of the magazine, Ms. Mary Ann O'Roark, said in an interview, that the readers of the magazine found great strength and support from the real life stories they published. One of these stories was about a former beauty queen and winner of the Miss America contest, Jackie Townsend, who was afflicted with a severe paralytic stroke in her early twenties. The stroke left her unable to walk, talk or communicate in any way with the world outside. But Miss Townsend turned inward and found great comfort in her inner love for God. Her faith sustained her in her loneliness and disability. It was only much later that she was able to relearn and resume her normal functions and when this miracle of healing happened, she was happy to share her experiences with the readers of *Guideposts*. Her story drew several emotional responses from the readers, overwhelming Ms. O'Roark, the editor.

"With all the increased interest in technology and other things," Ms. O'Roark remarked, "we thought we could find happiness in money, status and material possessions; and we have learnt that hey, that is not so! All those things do not bring abundant living. They do not give us true peace. People are now looking back and asking what can bring them peace and content. And they are finding that spiritual faith is the answer!"

Faith is the Key! A Recap for You:

1. Faith is nothing but optimism which leads to achievement.
2. Faith alone answers all questions, solves all problems and surmounts all sorrow and suffering, through courage and right attitude.
3. Faith is not mere emotionalism. It is not easy. Courage is required to cultivate faith.
4. Faith is the culmination of intense love and affection for God.
5. Faith may be cultivated through the Little Way – of good association, self-analysis, meditation, selfless service and constant prayer.
6. The trauma of uncertainty, stress and unhappiness can be conquered through faith and devotion.

Chapter 3

The Power is Within You

Gurudev Sadhu Vaswani often said to us, "You are not a weakling as some of you imagine yourselves to be. In you is a hidden *Shakti,* an energy, that is of Eternity."

The word *shakti* is derived from the Sanskrit root, "to be able". It is translated as, "Power, energy". In Hindu belief, it is the active power or manifest energy of Lord Siva that pervades all of existence. Scholars tell us that in its most refined aspect, it is *Parashakti* or pure consciousness. This pristine, divine energy unfolds as *ichha shakti* (the power of desire, will, love), *kriya shakti* (the power of action) and *jnana shakti* (the power of wisdom, knowing), represented as the three prongs of Siva's *trishula,* or trident. A divine spark of this supreme energy lies within each one of us, and is ours to tap.

"The energy of the mind is the essence of life," said Aristotle. The energy of the mind is only one half of the story; for the energy of the spirit is far more potent, far more powerful.

Our ancient rishis have also taught us about this tremendous power or *shakti* within us. Once this *shakti* is awakened, there is nothing that we cannot achieve. All we need to do is to tap our own spiritual strength.

During the troubled days following the traumatic partition of India, Sadhu Vaswani urged the refugees from Sind to be strong within. He exhorted them to be self sufficient and refrain from begging for government help. Again and again, he repeated those magic words which became a *mantra* of positive thinking for all of us: "Within you lies a hidden *shakti*; awaken that *shakti* and all will be well with you." I remember, too, his unforgettable call to the shattered community, "Believe and achieve."

I once read the story of a beggar. He lived under a tree. He sat there through rain and sunshine, day and night, summer and winter. He was homeless and lived in abject poverty. He ate whatever people threw into his begging bowl. One day he fell ill; his body was racked by pain and fever. He had no money to buy medicine or go to a doctor for treatment. He lay under the tree, ill and delirious until death released his soul from his wasted, emaciated body. A life of utter destitution had come to an end. The municipal workers accorded him the last dignity of a destitute's funeral. He had left the world, unwept, unhonoured, and unlamented.

A few days passed. The plot of land which he had made his home was acquired by a construction company in order to build a commercial complex. Heavy equipment was brought to dig the ground and lay the foundation for a huge building. When they had dug deep under the tree, the construction workers found a pot filled with silver and gold coins. This poor beggar had been literally sitting on a pot of gold; yet he had lived a life of utter deprivation. He was unaware of the treasure he was sitting on!

Are we not like that destitute beggar? An enormous treasure of *shakti* lies locked and hidden within us. But we go through life, without ever unfolding this *shakti,* without using it for our own betterment. Little do we realise that within us is the hidden potential that can transform our lives. There is a Power house within us and still we live in a state of permanent power failure!

In the Bhagavad Gita, Sri Krishna tells Arjuna, "O Arjuna, I reside in every heart". In each one of us is the Divine Spirit. Just imagine, the Almighty, the power Supreme dwells within us. Each one of us is a potent Krishna. Yet we live like weaklings. At the slightest difficulty, before the smallest obstacle, we retreat, we give way and break down. We succumb to pressures and problems, we get caught in a vicious circle of desires. It is sad, that despite the great '*Shakti*' of Krishna within us, we despair and fall into melancholy.

"Ye are gods," Jesus said to the Jews. "Your substance is that of God Himself," said the Sufi teacher. "Whoso knows himself has light," said Lao Tse, the Chinese seer.

We are so obsessed, overcome by the material world of *maya* that we fail to realise this Divinity within us.

That is why our Rishis urge us to know ourselves well.

Sadhu Vaswani, repeatedly urged us, 'Awaken the *shakti* within you.' He opened an *Ashram* in Rajpur and named it 'The *Shakti Ashram*'. He opened another ashram in South India and called it, '*Para Shakti Ashram*'. He urged the youth to be strong, to awaken the *shakti* within; to be brave and accept the challenges of life, to tap the 'power house' of infinite energy within them.

The question is: how can we awaken this *shakti*? How may we go deep within the self and kindle the source of this *shakti*?

Consider Mahatma Gandhi. He was an ordinary man like you and me. But he had awakened the inner *shakti*, and hence he could wage a successful battle, a battle without any weapons, a battle without bloodshed, against the mighty British Empire. What was this inner *shakti* all about? What was it that made Mahatma Gandhi a great hero?

Gandhi stated that the most important battle to fight was overcoming his own demons, fears, and insecurities. In his own words, he tells us how he did it:

> When doubts haunt me, when disappointments stare me in the face, and when I see not one ray of light on the horizon, I turn to the Bhagavad Gita, and find a verse to comfort me; and I immediately begin to smile in the midst of overwhelming sorrow. My life has been full of tragedies and if they have not left any visible

and indelible effect on me, I owe it to the teachings of the Bhagavad Gita.

Shortly before he became President of the United States, Senator Barack Obama had this to say about the Mahatma:

> Throughout my life, I have always looked to Mahatma Gandhi as an inspiration, because he embodies the kind of transformational change that can be made when ordinary people come together to do extraordinary things. That is why his portrait hangs in my Senate office: to remind me that real results will come not just from Washington, but from the people.

The first thing we must do in order to awaken this kind of *shakti,* is to turn the mind inward, towards this powerhouse within us. The more willing we are to tap this energy within us, the more power will flow through us.

Truly has it been said, "Nothing splendid has ever been achieved except by those who dared believe that something inside of them was superior to circumstance."

To explain this ancient concept through a modern metaphor, I give you the words of a recent writer; "We are all such a waste of our potential, like three-way lamps using one-way bulbs."

Awaken the spiritual power within you! This is the true meaning of self reliance.

There is an interesting episode narrated in the *Bhagawat Purana*. Long ago there lived a King. A Pandit used to go to him every day and read the *Bhagawata* aloud. After every chapter, the Pandit would read the closing message, which said: he who religiously reads the *Bhagawata* or hears it, will himself witness the light and will achieve *mukti,* liberation from the cycle of birth and death.

After a few months of daily reading, when the Pandit had completed reading the *Bhagawata*, the King asked him a question, "Tell me, have I witnessed the light? Have I reached the stage where I will be released from the cycle of birth and death?" To this, the Pandit replied, "That is the question which you alone can answer for yourself, your majesty."

The King was not happy with this reply. "You have deceived me," he accused the Pandit. "Every evening, I have been hearing the *Bhagawat Purana.* At the end of each chapter you have said to me that he who hears the *Bhagawat Purana* will attain *mukti* and witness the light. Now, you have to prove what you have been reading. I give you one week's time to prove that I have attained liberation. If you fail to prove this, I will send you to the gallows."

The Pandit was taken aback. He had expected praise and reward from the King. Instead he had received a threat of death! Depressed, he returned home. Six days passed by, but he could not find any solution to the problem. How was he to prove to the king that after listening to the *Bhagawat Purana*, a man achieves *mukti?* The Pandit became worried and despondent.

His seven year old daughter, seeing her father's anguished face, asked him, "Baba, why are your eyes glistening with unbidden tears? What is your problem?"

The Pandit opened out his heart to his child. The girl heard him out. Then she said very innocently, "Is that what worries you? Don't cry, for I will come with you to the King's *darbar* tomorrow, and I will explain the situation to the King and hopefully convince him."

On the following day, the girl accompanied the Pandit to the King's palace. On entering the *darbar* she ran to one of the ornamental pillars and embraced it. And then, she began to cry at the top of her voice, "O please, please, will someone release me from the grip of this pillar? This pillar is holding me." The King witnessed the scene from his throne and thought that the girl was indeed stupid. Who has brought this foolish child to the court, he wondered. Surely, she was mad. For she herself was clinging to the pillar and shouting to others to come and rescue her!

Aloud, he said to her, "Oh foolish girl, just leave that pillar." The girl cried still louder, "O please, please, separate me from this pillar. Come someone, I have to go back home, but the pillar will not let me go. Have mercy on me and please release me from the clutch of this pillar."

Now the King was really angry. "Who is this stupid girl?" he thundered. "Who has brought her here to my palace? I shall punish them both severely."

On hearing this, the girl left the pillar with a smile. She humbly bowed before the King and said to him, "Your Majesty, you too are holding on to the pillar of your ego. You are unnecessarily blaming my father for not having achieved *mukti*. Leave the ego and you will surely witness the light."

The King realised his mistake. He saw that *mukti* is not a gift which someone could present to him on a platter. *Mukti* is to be earned. The saints, sages and the scriptures can only show us the path, but it is we who have to walk the path.

No one will 'grant' you spirituality, no one can present spiritual strength to you. Your spiritual energy has to develop from within. It is you yourself who must grow and evolve in spiritual strength in order to make a success of your life on earth and in the dimension beyond.

Let me tell you about a *dervish* (a holy man). He was a poor man, who worked hard during the day to earn his living and studied late into the night. It was his desire to be well educated. He would burn the midnight oil, both literally and metaphorically, for he used to read by the light of an oil lamp. One night, when he sat down to read, he realised that he had run out of oil. He could not get it from anywhere at that late hour. Disappointed, he went to sleep, regretting that the night had been wasted.

That night he had a dream. In the dream Prophet Mohammed appeared before him and said to him, "Do not be dejected my child, do not be sad. Just open your mouth and I will pour the wisdom of the world into it.

You will be the wisest among men." Do you know what the *dervish* replied? In the dream the young *dervish* replies, "I do not want you to gift me knowledge. All I want is a little oil for my lamp so that I can study. I do not want knowledge without effort. I want to learn and study and gain knowledge through my own effort."

What a splendid example for us to emulate! Truly has it been said that the man who acquires the ability to take full possession of his own mind may take possession of anything else to which he is justly entitled.

In this connection, I am reminded of one of those delightful stories of Mullah Nasruddin. Once, a group of men from the Mullah's village decided to set out in search of God. The whole village gathered to see them off on their journey. A few minutes after they had left, the villagers saw Nasruddin riding out at a tearing speed on his donkey.

"Stop! Stop, Nasruddin, and tell us where you are off to!" they called after him.

"Don't ask me anything now," said Nasruddin. "I'm on a very important mission. When I come back, I'll tell you all about it."

He rode his donkey post-haste until he caught up with the pilgrims. Then he hastily dismounted from the donkey and greeted them.

"What has brought you here in such speed?" the pilgrims demanded. "Is it that you have decided to join us in our quest?"

"I would, indeed, love to go with you," said Nasruddin, still panting from the ride. "But I can't find my donkey. If I did, I would join you right away!"

"Don't be absurd, Nasruddin," said one of the pilgrims. "Why, you came here riding on your donkey – and you claim that you are looking for him!"

"If I am absurd, brother, only consider how ridiculous all of you are! You have set out on a pilgrimage in search of God – and He is right there, within you!"

As seekers, we are looking for what is within us – what we need is an arousal of consciousness.

"What lies behind us and what lies before us are tiny matters compared to what lies within us," said Emerson. Instead of constantly worrying about what may happen and what we may not achieve, let us look within, to tap these hidden powers that are ours by right!

Alas, we estimate our weaknesses all too well; but we never ever learn about the powers we have within us!

We must remember too, that there can be no true gain without pain. The energy within us must be channelised into meaningful, constructive action. Let us earn our own merit; let us achieve our heart's desires with effort and hard work. What we achieve through our own effort, can never be snatched away from us. Therefore, let us awaken the *shakti* within: let us grow in spiritual strength and be blessed.

Think about it...

Faith and belief comprise a very important part of our lives. A person's beliefs define who they are — how they see themselves, what they want out of life, and more.

We all have the power within us to be the best and the most powerful we can be. Through self awareness and spiritual awakening we can achieve anything and everything we ever wanted. To understand the powers of the universe and how to attract exactly what we want into our lives, all you need do is BELIEVE.

Janice M. Pickett

Our deepest fear is not that we are inadequate. Our deepest fear is that we are powerful beyond measure. It is our light, not our darkness that most frightens us. We ask ourselves, 'Who am I to be brilliant, gorgeous, talented, fabulous?' Actually, who are you not to be? You are a child of God. Your playing small does not serve the world. There is nothing enlightened about shrinking so that other people won't feel insecure around you. We are all meant to shine, as children do. We were born to make manifest the glory of God that is within us. It's not just in some of us; it's in everyone. And as we let our own light shine, we unconsciously give other people permission to do the same. As we are liberated from our own fear, our presence automatically liberates others.

— Marianne Williamson
(*A Return to Love: Reflections on the Principles of a Course in Miracles*)

The Power Within: A Recap for you:

1. Within each one of us is a hidden *'Shakti'*, which means "ability", which translates to 'energy' or 'power'- of desire, of action, of wisdom.
2. We should tap into our own spiritual strength and realise the Divinity within us.
3. The solution to every problem lies within you. Turn the mind inward and make your life anew.
4. With the help of God discover the latent power within you; recognise your true potential and overcome the limitations and restrictions of human existence and its environment.
5. Spirituality cannot be 'granted'. One has to grow and evolve in spiritual strength through one's own efforts.

Chapter 4

FAITH IS NOT AN OCCULT POWER

In the past, many Westerners regarded India as an 'exotic' nation of the 'Orient' – and both those adjectives had the wrong connotations for them. Fed on a diet of 'exotic' fiction, they regarded India as a land of snake charmers, half-crazed ascetics, pseudo-yogis who lay on beds of nails, and men who levitated on *padmasanas.*

My readers who are proud to regard the India of the twenty-first century as the super power of the future and the knowledge capital of the emerging IT industry, will no doubt be put off by such blatant prejudice. But I assure you, such prejudices did exist in the past, with or without reason.

Let me also add another unpalatable fact: such feats as I have described above, were equated with 'yogic' powers and *siddhis*, and actually attributed to the Hindu way of life!

I want to make it clear at the very outset that when I urge you to release the *shakti* within you, I do *not* refer to such occult powers. The faith that I wish to inculcate in you, has nothing to do with these occult powers.

I do not deny that there are occult powers. Even today, there are people who practise these occult powers. Westerners are no exception to this. The cult of the 'kabbala' is one such popular group. The Noble Laureate W. B. Yeats, claimed that his mystical, philosophical work, *A Vision*, was based wholly on the 'automatic' writings of his wife, Georgie Lee Hyde. When I say 'automatic', I mean involuntary, unconscious writing which happens when the writer is actually in a trance-like state. To give you another example of occult powers, even today, people in east and west, are fascinated by séance sessions with a 'medium' who can communicate with the souls of the dead. Even today, there are people who can 'materialise' things out of thin air. There are people who are buried alive in locked and chained trunks and make good their release.

Supernatural powers are mentioned in our ancient scriptures and are referred to as *ashta siddhis*. The Theosophy Dictionary defines these as "the eight supernormal powers or faculties innate in man but at present generally latent or undeveloped, although attainable when a person reaches the status of a *buddha*."

I have met a few people with such supernormal powers or *siddhis,* as they are called. But rather than relate my experiences, I would like to share with you an incident narrated by Swami Vivekananda, in one of his letters to Ajit Singh, the Maharaja of Khetri.

Swamiji was travelling in South India at that time, and happened to be told about a man who could read people's thoughts. Accompanied by a few friends, Swamiji went to see the man, who was a poor, unpretentious trader. Before they left on the visit, they consulted with each other, and thought of three sentences which they would test him with: Swamiji chose a *mantra* in Sanskrit, *Om Namo Bhagavate Vasudevaya.* His friend chose a Tibetan aphorism from the Buddhist scriptures. This way, they felt, the occult powers of the man would be comprehensively tested, for he was not likely to be familiar with any of the languages in question.

They were told that the man was in no mood to take on any visitors that day. But when he saw Swamiji, the man immediately requested him to give him some holy ash (*vibhuti*), for he had been feeling quite ill, after the visit of a few European visitors the previous day; he told Swamiji that he suspected those visitors of giving him '*drishti dosh*' or the evil eye, as we call it in India. However, all would be well with him if Swamiji gave him *vibhuti.*

Swamiji protested that he himself had no powers of *siddhi;* but the man said to him that he knew better, and that Swamiji should simply give him the holy ash as desired. When Swamiji obliged, the man surprised him by asking, "Being a *sannyasi,* you are still thinking of your mother, aren't you?" Swamiji was taken aback, for his thoughts were constantly dwelling on his mother at that time! The man wrote something on a chit of paper and gave it to the visitors. Later, when they asked him to tell them the lines that they had chosen to concentrate on, he told them to open the chit of paper he had given to them. And they found the lines – in Sanskrit and Tibetan – actually written out in the chit, by this man who had never left his village in South India, and had no knowledge of any one of those languages!

Swamiji concludes his narration by quoting from Shakespeare: "More things are wrought in heaven and earth, than are dreamt of in your philosophy."

Swamiji himself was a witness to these occult powers. He concluded that it is possible to cultivate such powers through concentration, *mantra japa* and other yogic practices. But I wish to stress again, that the faith I wish to inculcate does not involve the use of such powers.

It is said that one day, Sri Ramakrishna Paramahansa narrated to his disciples the parable of a man, who, after fourteen years of intense *sadhana* in a forest, acquired the *siddhi* of walking on water. He tried the feat again and again, to ensure his mastery over it – and each time, he succeeded effortlessly. Overjoyed with his *siddhi,* he rushed to his Guru and exclaimed, "Oh Gurudev, I can now walk over the waters as easily as others walk upon the earth."

His Guru smiled and said to him, "Pray, tell us how long it took you to acquire this power?"

Bursting with pride, the man answered, "Not one, not two, not ten, but fourteen long years did I spend in this *tapoban,* undertaking the most severe austerities and penance to acquire this *siddhi."*

And the Guru said to him, "Fie on you! Fourteen years of your precious life have you wasted in acquiring a power, for which the poorest peasant pays just one *paisa* – for that is exactly the amount one pays to the boatman who ferries you across the river! What a price you have paid to gain this one *paisa* worth of power!"

All the great spiritual teachers of humanity have effectively discouraged their disciples from practising occult powers. In truth, *siddhis* often become a distraction, a diversion from the path of spiritual growth. Therefore, are we urged to keep away from these occult powers.

One of Sri Ramakrishna's own disciples came to him and said, "Master, I have acquired the *siddhi* of reading people's minds. Merely by looking at a person, I can tell you what is going on in his mind."

"Shame on you!" said Sri Ramakrishna to the man. "Of what use is it to dig into such filth? Give up this horrible practice, and walk on the straight and narrow path that leads you to your Divine Mother!"

The straight and narrow path that leads us to our own Divine Mother is the path of faith! This is the way I would like my friends to walk.

When the great Tibetan yogi Milarepa was a young lad, his widowed mother and her young children were unscrupulously cheated by their father's family. The considerable wealth left to them by their father was appropriated by his brother and sister, while Milarepa's family was reduced to utter poverty.

Their mother was heartbroken at the misfortune that had befallen them. Her grief and misery hardened her heart to such an extent, that she was crazy to seek revenge on the relatives who had cheated her children of their inheritance.

When Milarepa was fifteen years old, she said to him, "You owe it to your father and me, to wreak vengeance on those wicked people who have reduced us to such utter penury. I now command you to go to a sorcerer and acquire occult powers and the art of magic from him through your diligence and effort. My heart and soul will not be at peace until you return and teach a lesson to those who cheated and betrayed us."

Milarepa obeyed his mother. In fact, he was such an earnest and apt pupil that he mastered the art of black magic thoroughly, and actually brought about the utter ruin and death of all the wicked people who had defrauded his mother. But the consequences for him were far reaching. He became deeply repentant at all the death and destruction which he had caused. He felt that he had taken on a heavy debt of bad *karma,* which he would never be able to repay in a million lives!

That is a long story, which I cannot relate now. Suffice it to say that Milarepa renounced all the occult powers he had mastered and sought refuge at the feet of a guru, who could wipe out all the negative effects of his bad *karma.* He achieved the freedom he sought after a great struggle and ordeal.

Even today, there are many men and women who claim to have reached the pinnacle of *siddhis* and *yogic* feats. They proclaim themselves to be 'God' men. People flock to them – for people are desperate to find light – and they are swept off their feet by impressive 'rituals' and mysterious acts and feats which they are made to 'witness'.

There was a time when voodoo, black magic and drug-induced visions were offered to Western seekers who were 'seeking' a solution to their problems. This only had a retrograde effect on such 'seekers' – it led to their mental and physical imbalance, without touching their spirit in the least.

Gurudev Sadhu Vaswani believed – and also taught us to believe – that one's spiritual *shakti* should not be channelised into performing extraordinary deeds for the sake of demonstrating such power. And so I would say – No, you cannot recognise a true Guru by the 'extraordinary' deeds that he performs.

The true seeker must understand once and for all not to confuse the occult and the exotic with true spirituality. You cannot go 'window shopping' for a Guru to teach you occult powers in a spiritual market place; you cannot look for a Guru on special offer for 'feats' in the Mall of Realisation. Although at times, it looks to us as if we can take our pick from the various 'cults', 'practices', 'theories' and 'rituals' that are piled up for our choice, we must not be led away by externals. It is essential to remember that the Truth we seek is *within* ourselves – and that this power has nothing to do with trying to impress others!

For Your Reflection...

"Once upon a time, a *sadhu* acquired great occult powers. He was vain about them. But he was a good man and had some austerities to his credit. One day the Lord, disguised as a holy man, came to him and said, 'Revered sir, I have heard that you have great occult powers.' The *sadhu* received the Lord cordially and offered him a seat. Just then an elephant passed by. The Lord, in the disguise of the holy man, said to the *sadhu*, 'Revered sir, can you kill this elephant if you like?'

"The *sadhu* said, 'Yes, it is possible.' So saying, he took a pinch of dust, muttered some *mantras* over it, and threw it at the elephant. The beast struggled awhile in pain and then dropped dead. The Lord said: 'What power you have! You have killed the elephant!' The *sadhu* laughed. Again the Lord spoke: 'Now can you revive the elephant?' 'That too is possible', replied the sadhu. He threw another pinch of charmed dust at the beast. The elephant writhed about a little and came back to life.

"Then the Lord said: 'Wonderful is your power. But may I ask you one thing? You have killed the elephant and you have revived it. But what has that done for you? Do you feel uplifted by it? Has it enabled you to realise God?' Saying this the Lord vanished.

"Subtle are the ways of *dharma*. One cannot realise God if one has even the least trace of desire. A thread cannot pass through the eye of a needle if it has the smallest fibre sticking out.

"Krishna said to Arjuna, 'Friend, if you want to realise Me, you will not succeed if you have even one of the eight occult powers.' This is the truth. Occult power is sure to beget pride, and pride makes one forget God."

Sri Ramakrishna Paramahansa

Faith Is Not An Occult Power: Recap for you:

1. Faith should not be confused with occult powers or accomplishments.
2. The development and practise of *'siddhis'* or occult powers have been discouraged by the great spiritual teachers of humanity. They are a diversion from the path of spiritual growth.
3. The straight and narrow path of faith leads us to our own Divine Mother.

Chapter 5

The Secret of Triple Faith

Swami Vivekananda said to us: "Never think there is anything impossible for the soul. It is the greatest heresy to think so. If there is sin, this is the only sin – to say that you are weak, or others are weak."

Truly has it been said: "With God's grace you can sail over the seven seas and cross over the seven mountains. Without His grace, you cannot even cross your threshold."

What is there that we cannot do with God's grace? With faith in God, you can move mountains. With faith in God, the impossible becomes quite possible for you. All you need is – faith in yourself, faith in the universe around you, and faith in the Almighty Power whom for want of a better word we call God.

I set special store by this triple faith – faith in the self; faith in the universe around us, and faith in God. This triple faith can lead you to great heights.

Think of the Wright Brothers and their remarkable achievement. People had dreamed of flying for many years. The United States Army had been trying to develop an airplane for a long time, but they could not succeed in making it fly. Commenting on their failure, *The New York Times* wrote that maybe in one million to ten million years they might be able to make a plane that would fly!

Only eight days later two men were successful in flying the first manned plane. They were Wilbur Wright and his younger brother, Orville. They had made a propeller-driven airplane and it had stayed in the air for just twelve seconds! But it made history. It was called the Wright Flyer. They made three more flights that day at Kitty Hawk, North Carolina. Only five people were there to see the flights, and very few newspapers even wrote a story about it.

As youngsters, they learned to enjoy 'tinkering' with mechanical things from their mother, who was always fixing and repairing things. The boys earned money by making home-made mechanical toys. When bicycles became popular, they opened a bicycle shop. They studied birds and how they flew. They experimented with kites, gliders and other flying machines. They contacted other people who were trying to fly. They made a wind tunnel at their shop to test different kinds of wings.

They continued to work on their planes and improve them constantly; and five years after that historical first flight, Orville took off on his machine, and remained in the air for one hour and two minutes. Wilbur and Orville Wright achieved an extraordinarily difficult technical goal that had eluded engineers for over a century. The airplane, a product of their combined inventive genius, would reshape the history of the twentieth century. They believed in themselves; they had faith in God; they had faith in the world around them. With this triple faith they created history.

"On May 29, 1953, Edmund Hillary of New Zealand and Tenzing Norgay of Nepal became the first human beings to conquer Mount Everest – Chomolungma, to its people – at 29,028 ft. the highest place on earth," reported *Time* magazine. By any rational standards, this was no big deal. Aircraft had long before flown over the summit, and within a few decades literally hundreds of other people from many nations would climb Everest too. And what is particularly remarkable, anyway, about getting to the top of a mountain?" asked *Time* Magazine, before setting out to answer that question themselves.

"Geography was not furthered by the achievement, scientific progress was scarcely hastened, and nothing new was discovered. Yet the names of Hillary and Tenzing went instantly into all languages as the names of heroes, partly because they really were men of heroic mold but chiefly because they represented so compellingly the spirit of their time," the magazine wrote.

> Hillary and Tenzing were two cheerful and courageous fellows doing what they liked doing, and did, best, and they made an oddly assorted pair. Hillary was tall, lanky, big-boned and long-faced, and he moved with an incongruous grace, rather like a giraffe. He habitually wore on his head a homemade cap with a cotton flap

behind, as seen in old movies of the French Foreign Legion. Tenzing was by comparison a Himalayan fashion model: small, neat, rather delicate, brown as a berry, with the confident movements of a cat. Hillary grinned; Tenzing smiled. Hillary guffawed; Tenzing chuckled. Neither of them seemed particularly perturbed by anything; on the other hand, neither went in for unnecessary bravado.

When Tenzing reached the summit, he buried a few offerings that he had brought with him, into the virgin snow. It was a Sherpa gesture of thanksgiving to the Lord and to Mother Nature.

They became household names, heroes of humanity overnight. They achieved their rare feat with the power of triple faith! As Time magazine put it, "By conquering Everest, the beekeeper and the Sherpa affirmed the power of humble determination – and won one for underdogs everywhere!"

"Faith is the cornerstone of all," Sri Ramakrishna asserted.

Our ancient scriptures, the Vedas, also teach us to be at peace with ourselves, the universe we live in, and the Almighty who rules over us all.

There was a time when such a harmony came naturally to mankind. They venerated the *panchabhutas* or the five elements; they venerated Nature and treated every aspect of God's creation with love and reverence; they lived at peace with their fellow men.

This sense of harmonious living in the universe is expressed in the *Shanti Sukta* from the *Atharva Veda*:

Om Shanta dhyou
Shanta prithvi
Shantam idam urantharikısham
Shanta udhanvatirapa
Shantana sant aushadi

May peace prevail in the skies
May peace prevail on earth
May peace prevail in vast space
May peace prevail in the flowing river, and in plants and trees!

I cannot help wondering whether we have lost this sense of living in harmony with Nature! From reverence for the universe, we have turned to arrogance in our own power; from veneration of nature, we have turned to exploitation of the abundant resources of Nature; and now, we talk of colonising space . . .

A friend pointed out to me that large tracts of the plains of North India are now becoming devoid of groundwater reserves. Who would have thought this possible in the land washed by the Ganga, Yamuna, Saraswati, Sarayu and the other sacred rivers?

I was deeply saddened to read of the suicides of hundreds of farmers across the length and breadth of the country. Why were these sons of the soil let down by the land which they had considered as their own mother?

We know that the fishing communities of the South were worst affected by the tsunami of 2003. Why did the sea god, who was like their own father, betray these humble fisher folk?

A few years ago, over two hundred pilgrims from India who were on a sacred pilgrimage to Manasarovar and Mount Kailash in Tibet, were caught in an avalanche, and tragically lost their lives. Why did it happen that these pious people were let down by the very forces of Nature whom they wished to worship?

The answer is not far to seek: we, the people, failed to keep our faith with the universe we live in. We failed to keep faith with the Mother Nature; we failed to keep faith with the deep seas, the majestic mountains and the life-sustaining rivers of this ancient land. We caused the erosion of the coastline with uncontrolled, unregulated illegal constructions. We caused deforestation of the green mountain slopes with our greed for more and more land to build on; we caused the unimaginable pollution of the rivers with our brutal, ruthless urge to treat this planet like one vast garbage dump!

We can see it in the way we treat the soil; we can see it in the way we have destroyed the habitat of wild animals; we can see it in the pollution of our waterways, the degradation of our environment, the depletion of the ozone layer and the complete and utter waste of Mother Nature's resources.

Although I said "Mother Nature," I doubt if we have the right to call ourselves her children anymore! We are actually a vital component of nature, and it is our sacred obligation to preserve and protect this planet that God has given to us as a habitat. Alas, we live upon earth as if there is no tomorrow—as if we care nothing for unborn generations who will continue to live here long after we are gone!

We failed to keep our faith – and we paid the price!

The universe gives us in return for what we give to it. We cannot claim to love the universe and continue to treat it as if it were our lumber room!

When man reveres and respects cosmic laws, when man realises that it is God's power that is manifested in the universe around him, and when he cultivates the faith to make all his efforts and achievements an offering to this Almighty Power – then truly, man has built up the triple faith that is a requisite for all success.

Without this triple faith, nothing is possible. With it, nothing is impossible!

"Where does God and the universe come into the picture?" some of you might ask. "It's I, me, my life, my effort, my work, my achievement. Why do I have to drag the Cosmic powers into my personal world?"

The answer to that question is this: the same *shakti* that is present within you, is manifested in the workings of this vast universe. The One Life animates all Creation; and that life energy comes from God, who is the Creator of the entire universe and the Bestower of all that we have. When we link ourselves to the power and energy of the universe, our own finite power and energy are multiplied manifold.

Think of yourself opening the windows of your room early in the morning, and breathing in deeply, the fresh, cool, invigorating morning air.

Think of all those men and women who rise early to take a pre-dawn walk on the beach, often ending with a *suryanamaskar*.

Think of a tired teacher or researcher, putting her reading/writing work away for a few minutes, to look up at the clean blue sky and refresh her eyes and her mind.

Think of the business magnates in South Mumbai who snatch precious minutes from their hectic schedules to go jogging on the promenade at Nariman Point or at the Bandstand in Bandra.

Think of the Puneite who allots at least one weekend a month to go on a trek up the green Sahyadris.

Think of the busy New Yorker who juggles his routine to be able to spend a few minutes at the Central Park.

All these people have one thing in common: they are recharging their spirits by contact with the refreshing energy of the universe.

Unlike the human mind, the universe does not emit negative energies. Sunshine or rain, calm or storm, morning or night, the universe is always a store house of marvelous positive energy.

We have often heard of people saying, "I've been cooped up in my office all day, and I have a headache," or "I've been pouring over my accounts for hours, and I'm exhausted." Have you ever heard people complaining, "I've just come back from a walk and I feel drained out"; or "I have taken a stroll in the park and I am suffering from a headache"?

The positive forces of Nature, the life-giving energy of this Universe is meant to revive us, restore us to emotional and physical balance, and revive our flagging spirits. We must tap this energy if we wish to achieve the best that we are capable of.

Reverence for Nature is essential. Reverence for Nature will help us to survive upon this planet. Reverence for nature will help us to preserve and protect this blessed earth for our children—and our children's children.

Reverence is essential—reverence for our rivers and forests; reverence for our lakes and waterfalls; reverence for trees and plants and the grass that grows beneath our feet; reverence for birds and beasts, whom I love to call our younger brothers and sisters.

Gurudev Sadhu Vaswani spoke to us of the *Prakriti Sangha*—fellowship with nature—which he believed was essential to human happiness. There is a spiritual element in the beauty of nature, for Nature is God's own expression in all its joy. It is the song, the dance of the Lord. Nature is truly the environment of the *atman*—the eternal soul within each human being.

The Swiss psychiatrist Carl Jung states, "Civilisation today has become sick because man has alienated himself from God."

Is not this the worst malady that afflicts modern man? We live in an age of unprecedented scientific progress and technological development. Science has given us so many blessings, so many comforts, so many conveniences, so many gadgets. But alas, all this has only inflated our ego and blinded us to the truth about ourselves—that we are all God's children.

I think the greatest affliction of modern civilisation is that we are moving away from God, and the awareness that we are His children.

God is the source and sustainer of life. And man cannot live a healthy life physically, mentally, morally, spiritually, so long as he cuts himself off from God. It is very easy to drive the spirit out of the door—but once you have done that, life loses its flavor; the 'salt of life' grows flat.

Very many years ago, a young man came to meet Gurudev Sadhu Vaswani. He was utterly desolate and downcast, and he said to the Master, "I am just thirty years old, and I am an utter failure! I have lost my job. My ancestral property is mortgaged. My wife has left me, and I am unable to support my old mother. I am utterly frustrated with life. What shall I do?"

Gurudev Sadhu Vaswani said to him, "You are not the pathetic weakling that you take yourself to be! You are not poor and broken! You are like the prodigal son who has drifted away from his rich father and does not know how infinitely rich he is."

The young man was bemused. "Excuse me," he stammered. "Who is this rich father you are speaking of? My own father passed away five years ago—and he only left behind debts which I am yet to pay off!"

Sadhu Vaswani smiled and said to him, "I am speaking of our Heavenly Father. He is the Father of us all. And He is the source of all supply. He is the source of all that you and I will ever need or desire. He is the source of prosperity, plenty and peace. He is the source of happiness and harmony. He is the source of love and joy, strength and wisdom, power and security. All you need to do is turn to Him—and you will lack nothing!"

All we have to do is turn to Him – with absolute Faith in Him, with belief in ourselves and in the Universe He created.

How many of us are capable of this triple faith?

When you are in tune with nature, all weather is fine weather!

Sunshine is delicious, rain is refreshing, wind braces us up, snow is exhilarating; there is really no such thing as bad weather, only different kinds of good weather.

– John Ruskin

Let the rain kiss you. Let the rain beat upon your head with silver liquid drops. Let the rain sing you a lullaby.

– Langston Hughes

Rainbows apologise for angry skies.

– Sylvia Voirol

To be interested in the changing seasons is a happier state of mind than to be hopelessly in love with spring.

– George Santayana

The best thing one can do when it's raining is to let it rain.

– Henry Wadsworth Longfellow

For your reading pleasure:

In Tune With Mother Nature

If you listen for the songbirds
As they greet the summer sun,
And love the way the wind can make
The trees sing just for fun;

If you like to hear the ocean
As it drums upon the shore,
And imagine all the whales out there,
And hope they'll sing some more;

If you think of all the animals
As players in a band,
Each with a lovely tune to play,
All needed on the land;

And know that as a boy or girl
A woman or a man
You have a vital role to play
In Mother Nature's plan;

If you honor every living thing
As a part of nature's treasure
You're in tune with Mother Nature
So let's all sing her song together.

Courtesy: canteach.com

The Secret Of Triple Faith – Recap for You:

1. You can attain great heights through triple faith – faith in the self, faith in the universe around, and faith in God.
2. There are countless examples of individual achievements that affirm the power of humble determination through faith in the self.
3. The Sense of living in harmony with Nature is attained through reverence for the universe. When we fail to keep faith with the universe we live in, we pay a heavy price.
4. Man must realise that it is God's Power that is manifested in the universe around him. He must cultivate the faith to make his every act an offering to this Almighty Power.
5. The One life animates all creation. When we link ourselves to this life energy which comes from God our own finite power and energy are multiplied.
6. The greatest affliction of modern civilisation is moving away from God and the awareness being His children.

Chapter 6

The Mountains That Faith Must Move

Faith can move mountains!

You will agree with me that these are words that have inspired courage, confidence and optimism in hundreds and thousands of hearts since they were uttered, millennia before today...

Having read only recently of Hillary, Tenzing and the conquest of Mt. Everest, I hope my readers are not setting out for the Alps, the Rockies or the Himalayas, to command them to move in the Name of God!

Let me quote an anonymous saying to curb excessive enthusiasm on your part: "True, faith can move mountains: but don't be surprised if God hands you a shovel."

In other words, we must learn to pull and pray; for prayer with your personal effort is the true way of achievement. As a wise man tells us, "Your faith must allow God to be God." While you can certainly call for

His grace and help, you cannot sit back and expect Him to do your homework. If that is what you understood by faith – leaving it all to God while you sink into inertia and passivity – you need to relearn your concept of faith. In this, as in so many other things, it is good to remember that much loved proverb: God helps those who help themselves! As Edmund Hillary put it so well, "It is not the mountain we conquer but ourselves."

There is a beautiful story of which the great German poet Goethe was very fond. Peter asked Jesus, "How is it that you can walk on the waters, and we cannot?"

Jesus answered, "Because I have faith!"

Peter said, "We also have faith."

"Then follow me," said Jesus, and stepped on the water. Peter followed. They had not gone very far when a huge wave arose in the waters.

Peter cried, "Master, save me: I am sinking!"

"What is the reason?" asked Jesus.

And Peter said, "Master, I saw a huge wave and fear entered my heart."

Jesus said, "You feared the wave: You did not fear the Lord of the waves!"

With Faith you can witness miracles in your daily life – this is the message conveyed by Jesus.

To pious Hindus, the 'moving' of a mountain is not an unfamiliar thing. Did not Maha Vishnu oversee the uprooting of the mighty, legendary Mandaranchal mountain to be used as a 'whisk' to churn the ocean during the *samudra manthan?* Did not Sri Krishna lift the Govardhana Giri effortlessly to protect the *gopas* and *gopis* from the fury of Indra? And did not that great devotee of Sri Rama, the incomparable Rama Bhakta Hanuman move the Sanjivani Hill to the battlefield in Lanka to administer the healing medicinal herb that saved Lakshmana's life?

We know very well that God 'moved' these mountains. These incidents from our sacred *puranas* tell us that nothing is impossible if you have faith.

Let me narrate to you a Welsh legend. There was a tiny village standing near a small hillock in Wales. The villagers were proud of the historical legends associated with their tiny village. It was believed that Noah's Ark had landed on the flat top of their hillock, called Mt. Garth. However, their pride in their village took a severe beating when two government cartographers arrived in their village, and set out to measure Mt. Garth. After a preliminary survey, they brusquely told the villagers that their hill could not really be called a mountain, for it was not even 1000 ft. in height. The trouble was, the hillock was 'short' by about 100 feet or so.

Enterprising villagers, their friends and family members from far-flung areas, put their heads together. They would not allow two government geographers to deprive their village of its historical importance, by denying the name of 'mountain' to their own Garth. A plan was finalised – the villagers would *raise* the height of the mountain *physically* by piling up hard soil, rubble and stones on the flat hill-top.

The seemingly impossible scheme was executed and the government 'cartographers' were forced to conclude that Garth Hill was, in fact, a mountain.

So you see, the faith of the villagers actually caused a humble hill to become a mountain! As Andrew Carnegie once remarked, "The man who acquires the ability to take full possession of his own mind may take possession of anything else to which he is justly entitled."

But jests and stories apart, all of us are confronted by 'mountains' which thwart our progress and development, and become serious obstacles which impede our efforts.

What are these mountains? They are mountains of negativity – despair, defeatism, pessimism, low self-esteem, lack of self-confidence, guilt, inferiority complex, worry and anxiety!

These 'joy-killers' as I call them, must be thwarted, uprooted and set aside. If you are in a happy, light-hearted, positive frame of mind when you read this, you are likely to exclaim, "Surely, Dada is making a mountain of a mole-hill! Why do we need faith to get rid of negative impulses? A bit of exercise, a little positive thinking, a change of mood can surely do the trick!"

True, these 'joy-killers' are in reality mole-hills. But when we are in emotional turmoil and distress, these pathetic mole-hills assume the magnitude and formidable power of a 'mountainous' mental block!

Ask any student; he or she will tell you how they get into a 'writer's block'. They put pen to paper, and the ink may flow, but no words come out!

Ask any teacher; she will tell you her greatest fear is going 'blank' during a lecture.

Ask any businessman, and he will tell you the stress and tension he goes through before a transaction is successfully completed.

To quote William Shakespeare, "Our doubts are traitors, and make us lose the good we oft might win, by fearing to attempt." If there is a mountain, climb it! In the words of the Negro singer, go over it; go around it; or cut a tunnel through it!

Dear friends, these are minor matters compared to the crises people face during the course of their lives.

Think of a young wife whose hale and hearty husband is suddenly diagnosed with incurable cancer at a highly advanced stage.

Think of a mother who loses her first baby at childbirth.

Think of a family whose only breadwinner loses his job in a recession.

Think of a housewife who is confronted with the adultery of her husband.

Think of a soldier who loses his limbs during a 'routine' military exercise.

The truth is, that the mountain could be anything. The mountain might be a fatal disease in a loved one. Or it might be a crisis in your personal relationship. It might be a financial loss which threatens to ruin you. It is a mountain that seems to overwhelm you; it seems unmovable.

Ask any seasoned mountain-climber. He will tell you that the dedicated mountain climber is not intimidated by a mountain – he is inspired by it. So too, the true achiever is never discouraged by a problem – he is challenged by it. And so it is said: "Mountains are created to be conquered; adversities are designed to be defeated; problems are sent to be solved." With faith all this is possible.

As we proceed on the pathways of life, we face so many challenges and threats. Very often, we feel frightened. Life seems to be slipping out of our control. We must not forget that such experiences come to us, with a definite purpose. One great lesson which they teach us is to turn to God, to depend upon Him for everything. "Thou art at the helm, O Lord! And I have naught to fear. Thou wilt take care of Thy child!"

Calling upon God in times of trial and tribulation may appear to be a selfish act. All our acts, in the beginning, have to be selfish, until we grow in the spirit of detachment and learn to watch, as spectators, the ever-unfolding drama of life. If to rely upon God is to be selfish, it is far better to be 'selfish' than to be 'egoistic' and rely upon one's own limited powers. This 'selfishness' is a necessary step in our spiritual progress and will, at the right time, drop off on its own accord, even as the flower drops when the fruit is born.

The one lesson we all need to learn is utter dependence upon God. Everything else will follow. We must turn to God for every little thing we need until, one blessed day, we find that we need nothing; our one and only need is God! Then we make the great discovery that all we need is already provided for.

I am not asking you to treat God like your personal 'genie' who will execute all your desires as his commands! Having faith in God really means that you are ever ready to accept His Will in the assurance that He knows what is good for you, and is sure to give you whatever is good for you.

Pray for more and more faith. He who has faith has everything. For, verily, "faith moves mountains". Pray for faith as a famished person prays for food and a thirsty person for water. What is it to have faith? It is to feel sure that whatever God does is always for the best. It is to grow in the realisation that when God denies His child some good, He designs to give him something better.

Let me end with these beautiful lines that a friend sent to me:

> Only as high as I reach can I grow,
> Only as far as I seek can I go,
> Only as deep as I look can I see,
> Only as much as I dream can I be.

With faith in God, there is no height that you cannot reach; no distance that you cannot go; no dream that you cannot accomplish!

Did you know. . .

'Fire walking' or walking on live, hot coals is part of the festivities at many village temples in Tamil Nadu. Pious devotees whose prayers have been granted by the local deity often take a pledge that they would walk on fire to express their gratitude to the deity and to inculcate faith in others. This is a common feature in which young and old take part – and one which has been condemned as barbaric and blindly superstitious by rationalists.

The latest news is that 'fire-walking' has now become a routine exercise at some motivational seminars organised in the U.S. Participants are simply told that they can alter reality by the power of their faith and belief, and they do it to demonstrate that such faith can empower you and others!

How can you cultivate the kind of faith that you move mountains? How can you handle yourself and your life when difficulties strike?

In the pages that follow, I offer you a few practical suggestions which you might consider.

The Mountains that Faith Must Move... Recap for you:

1. Pull and Pray – God helps those who help themselves!
2. Nothing is impossible to those who act with faith.
3. Joy-killers which are molehills, often appear like mountains.
4. Mountains are created to be conquered.
5. Call upon God to create faith and strengthen faith!

Practical Suggestion No.

1

LEARN TO LET GO

The secret of true faith is in three words: "Let it go!" Let it go! Let go of your fears, your guilt, your problems and your frustrations. Let go in God's Name! For He is the Support and Sustenance of your life. There are no obstacles on your path that He cannot clear; no problems that He, in His Mercy and Wisdom cannot solve!

If you want to be at peace, if you want to feel that God is watching over your life, if you want to feel the abundant love of God in your heart, if you wish to live in the present moment, then just let go of all your anxieties and worries, let go of all the constraints which are oppressing you; hand your life over to God, and watch miracles happen!

Let go, let go, let God!

Sounds so simple doesn't it? And yet most of us know that this is not as easy as it sounds.

Peter Russel, an experimental psychologist who was the first in Britain to undertake research into the psychological effects of Meditation, believes that the essence of spiritual awakening is letting go. Here is his reflection on the subject:

Letting Go – How Difficult It Is

Years of personal experience,
combined with centuries of cultural learning,
have taught us the importance of holding on.

We hold on to our desires.
We hold on to what we think we need.
We hold on to what promises us happiness.

We hold on to our possessions.
We hold on to our image of who we are.
We hold on to our ideas of what is right.

We hold on to our theories.
We hold on to our beliefs.
We hold on to our attitudes.
We hold on to our judgements.

We hold on to the past
We hold on to the future.

We hold on to our grievances.
We hold on to our fears.

We hold on to our loves.
We hold on to our lovers.

We hold on to money.

We hold on to our thoughts.
We hold on to our illusions.

We hold on to our gods.
We hold on to our bodies.
We hold on to our lives.

So why do we hold on?...

Why do we hold on?

Indeed, it is a question that each of us must ask ourselves: why don't we let go? The answer could lie in attachment; or insecurity; or fear; or simply, the desire to control everything ourselves, even if it is having disastrous consequences!

Life is a roller coaster with its highs and lows, its ups and downs that sometimes propels us to dizzy heights and then pushes us into a precipitous fall. When the going is good, when we are on a 'high' as people call it, we enjoy the ride. When things begin to go wrong, we are apt to lose our balance. Failure and loss, disappointment and disruption of normalcy create negative emotions which soon express themselves in a mood of depression, gloom, despair and frustration.

Gurudev Sadhu Vaswani would often say to us that our so-called disappointments are His appointments, and that He upsets our plans only to set up His own – which are bound to be, in the long run, much better for us.

An effective way of dealing with despair and frustration is to go to the root of the matter, analyse and understand our own feelings and then to 'let go' of whatever is causing the destructive, negative emotion. Even if circumstances appear formidable and totally out of our control, it is important to remember that we can always choose to respond and react to the most adverse conditions in a positive and constructive way. In other words, our attitude is, and always should be, within our control. When we learn to cultivate such an attitude, we will find it far easier to face the challenges that life throws at us; above all, we become ready and willing to allow Divine guidance to lead us on the right path.

Life does not come to us with a special warranty. Change, as they say, is the only constant in life. Given this kind of uncertainty, the wise ones amongst us imbibe the valuable lesson that in this transient, impermanent life, everything passes away, sooner or later. That is why our sages and saints gave us the *mantra: this too shall pass away.*

The call to 'let go' is made by several faiths and their sacred scriptures, including that Universal Scripture, the Bhagavad Gita: "Renouncing all rites and writ duties, come to me for single refuge," Sri Krishna tells Arjuna. "Do not fear, for I shall save you from all bondage to suffering and sin."

Lao Tse, the great Chinese philosopher, once said, "Practise *not* doing and everything will fall into place". This does not literally mean 'do absolutely nothing', but rather that we should 'go with the flow' by accepting life as it comes, and living in the present moment, without constantly agonising about the past or worrying about the future. Lao Tse adds, "By strengthening your defense under adverse conditions, you will create an effective offense." And he writes, significantly: "When I let go of what I am, I become what I might be."

Vairagya (detachment), *samattvam* (equanimity), *sharanam* (surrender), these are the cardinal concepts of the Gita, and they all imply letting go. This sense of letting go is not passive inaction; it is dynamic acceptance of God's guiding, guarding power over us.

This is a true story that someone narrated to me. Two young women lived in a joint family. They were married to the two sons of the family, and were treated by all the members of the extended family as daughters-in-love, not as daughters-in-law. If the brothers were tied together by natural bonds of affection, the two sisters-in-love, Paro and Sita, were the best of friends, the closest of companions and a source of moral support and strength to each other at all times. When there was work to be done, they did it together, laughing and chatting. When there was leisure for relaxation, they enjoyed themselves, doing things together. They were virtually inseparable.

Paro had a diamond ring which had been given to her by her grandmother. It was her most precious possession, for she attached great sentimental value to it. She wore it on special occasions, and put it away carefully when she had to get back to housework. Sita often teased her about it, saying, "If you ask me, your smile is far more radiant than that ring of yours!"

One day, the family returned from a trip late in the evening. The children were hungry, and a meal had to be readied as quickly as possible. The sisters-in-law went straight to the kitchen and set about preparing food. Paro took away her diamond ring and put it on the kitchen window, and began to chop vegetables. Sita began to knead the dough for the *rotis*. As always, they worked well together, sharing the chores, laughing and chatting the while, as the delicious smell of cooking began to pervade the house.

Very soon, the food was on the table. Sita continued to roll out piping hot *rotis*, while Paro, the elder one, took the dishes out to feed the children and the aged parents-in-law. The brothers said they would eat later with their wives.

When the children and elders had eaten, the men helped their wives to bring the food to the table, and having said a prayer, they started to eat. Barely had she swallowed a morsel, when Paro exclaimed, "O Sita, my diamond ring! I left it on the kitchen window sill. Would you fetch it for me please?"

"Right away," laughed Sita. "I know you can't bear to be without it!" Walking into the kitchen, she called out a minute later, "Where did you leave it? It's not on the window."

"Look carefully," called out Paro. "I left it on the window sill."

Sita returned from the kitchen, "I'm telling you *didi*, it's not there!"

Paro went to the kitchen now. She stared at the window sill. It was wiped clean, empty. Her face turned pale, her heart turned dark. How could the ring disappear just like that? She had left it there barely an hour ago. And nobody had entered the kitchen except herself – herself … and Sita!

Paro came out. Her face was rigid with stress and anger. Wordlessly she took away her plate and washed it. The brothers stared at her in consternation. Sita was dismayed.

"*Didi,* why aren't you eating? Please have your dinner, and we'll look for the ring later. It can't have disappeared just like that!"

"Please do eat *bhabi*," said the younger brother. "You know this house is safe as a bank. Nothing has ever been lost here."

"Paro, please don't leave the table when all of us are about to eat," said her husband. "Can't you see how you are upsetting everyone!"

Paro flared up, "Can't you see how upset *I am*?" she cried and rushed out of the room. The others arose from the table. No one felt like eating. Sita cleared away the kitchen all alone. The brothers sat together quietly for sometime. Not a word was spoken.

Nearly an hour later, when Sita came out of the kitchen and switched off the lights, the elder brother said softly, "Don't worry, you two. Everything will be alright tomorrow. She is probably tired."

Everything was not alright next morning. Paro turned away when Sita came to see her next morning. She maintained a stony silence when Sita spoke to her. She refused to smile; refused to relent.

Her anger and hostility poisoned the atmosphere of the warm and comfortable family home. The old parents were heart broken by the sudden change in their elder daughter. The younger brother was distressed at the way his wife was being treated by Paro. The children were driven apart by the brewing feud between their mothers. For a month or two, life went on in a mechanical fashion. The sound of laughter vanished from the house.

Within two months, the younger brother had found himself a job in a Middle Eastern country. He told his parents, "It is in the family interest that I am leaving. You know how intolerable life has become for Sita after *bhabi* lost her ring. May be, if we go away, things will return to normal. After all, how long can *bhabi* continue to be angry?"

He was mistaken. Paro continued to be angry for years together. The old parents passed away; their sons were convinced they died of a broken heart. Paro had turned to stone. She snapped at the children; she never ever smiled.

Ten years later, Paro's husband died of a massive heart attack. His brother and Sita arrived from abroad. They tried to comfort Paro. But Paro turned her face away. The children were weeping aloud; but Paro maintained a stony silence.

Sita went to the kitchen to make tea. She set the water to boil and looked for the tea leaves and sugar. Everything was so strange and unfamiliar in the kitchen where she had once spent such happy, busy, fun-and-laughter filled hours!

As she fumbled to find the matches, she knocked off the sugar canister accidentally. Sugar spilled all over the kitchen floor. Paro came in, glaring at her. She snatched the broom from Sita's hand and began to sweep the floor angrily, aggressively, as if the room had been contaminated by Sita's presence. Furiously she brushed the spilled sugar away, as if trying to banish all the sweetness and joy of her past life. Under the shelves and cupboards she swept wildly, and a small object was hurled at Sita's feet. Paro looked up to see Sita pick it up and hold it wordlessly. It was Paro's grandmother's diamond ring.

Sita did not say a word. But Paro broke down completely. Years and years of pent up grief and sorrow and anger poured out of her embittered heart. The rest of the family rushed to the kitchen, and saw the strange tableau: Sita holding out a diamond ring, wordlessly; and Paro weeping as if her heart would break.

It was her brother-in-law who broke the impasse. "Let go, *bhabi*, let go," he said gently.

"Let go, let go," wept Paro. "Let go, let go! That's what your brother said to me over and over again, these past ten years. I was not prepared to let go! And now, he has gone, and I have let him depart without ever making up with him! And all because I was not prepared to let go! I lacked faith in our friendship; I lacked faith in my own husband; I lacked faith in God, and look what I'm reduced to now!"

Wordlessly, Sita took her hand and slipped the finger on her ring. The ring was so loose now, that it slipped and fell on the floor and rolled away once again.

"Let go, *didi*!" was all she could say.

The solution to most of our problems is to let go, in the Name of God. Trust to His wisdom, to solve your problems, when you feel that you can't cope, can't handle them yourself. It is particularly important to let go of petty resentments and losses. In the larger context of life, these issues are so petty and trivial. If you wish to nurture relationships, letting go of small irritations is a must. When you let go of your bitterness and anger, you will be surprised to realise how much more valuable life is, and how necessary it is to build lasting bonds with those you love.

The Tao philosopher, Sogyal Rinpoche says, "Learning to live is learning to let go," for nothing in life is permanent, he tells us; and eventually we have to let go of each and every thing that enters our lives, including ourselves. "Our minds busy our lives with their useless thoughts – the fears we have about the future, the torment that we have about our past, and the anxiety of what may or may not happen," he adds. "These very thoughts keep us spinning our wheels in our self-constructed whirlpool of negativity as we replay and rehearse situations of which we have no control. The more productive stance to take is, when we find ourselves in a useless battle, we merely walk off the battlefield."

Doctors are now telling us that letting go can cure us of serious ailments like ulcers, hypertension and cardio vascular diseases. Pessimism and cynicism are now perceived to be major inducements to a heart attack. Anger, envy, bitterness and hostility are also associated with heart attack risk. Psychiatrists tell us that Type A and Type D personalities are especially prone to illness, as both involve an inability to let go. The type A person is stressed and highly strung, while the type D person is always worried and anxious. By learning to let go of our cares, worries, anger, stress over deadlines and pressure of work, we may actually be lengthening our lives. We can certainly make life more worthwhile, more enjoyable, if we learn to let go!

Think about it...

It was a rain-drenched, stormy night on the Western Express Highway. One side of the highway had been closed due to a landslide, and vehicles crawled at a low speed on the open side. Dr. Patel's car was creeping up a steep incline behind ten other cars; they were all stuck behind a huge slow-moving truck which could not take the incline. Dr. Patel was hungry and exhausted; he was due at his destination at 8 pm for a business dinner, and it was already ten o'clock, and they were still crawling...

Dr. Patel cursed under his breath at the slow progress the truck was making. In normal circumstances, all the expensive and flashy cars including his own, would have simply whizzed past the lumbering truck without so much as a second thought. But on this stormy, dark night, with the oncoming traffic in the same lane, it was next to impossible! The driving rain made it difficult to see very far ahead.

Suddenly, the cars ahead of his began to zoom past the truck. Hopefully, Dr. Patel began to speed up, and as he moved forward, he could see that the truck driver was waving his hand vigorously, indicating that the cars behind him could move ahead and overtake him. Obviously, he could see that the way ahead was clear. As Dr. Patel sped past him, he raised his hand in a grateful gesture to the unknown driver.

He thought to himself, "I wonder where the truck is from... it might be from any corner of the country, east or west, north or south... that driver is a stranger to all of us who were stuck behind him for so long. And yet, all of us trusted him implicitly and moved ahead when he gave us the signal to go past. How safe to know that someone could see exactly what is ahead, and trust to his judgement!"

Steps to let go...

To make the process of letting go a little easier, there are two things you can do:

The first is trust. Trust that no matter what happens, you will be okay. Now this doesn't mean that life will turn out the way that you want it to. Life often doesn't. Trust is knowing that however life turns out, you will be fine.

When you know that you will be fine, no matter what happens, letting go becomes relatively easy. As you let go, you restore your effectiveness and life works out great. This then reinforces the trust.

When you don't trust, life becomes threatening. You fight, resist, hang on, and withdraw. You then make everything worse, which reinforces "don't trust."

Trust is actually a choice. Trust is something you create. It's a declaration. "I will be okay no matter what happens. I trust, just because I say so."

Trust is also telling the truth. You really will be fine no matter what happens. You have had difficult times before and you have made it through every one of them.

Life is only threatening when you resist. So stop resisting and trust. Trust that no matter what happens, you will be okay.

The second and most important step in the process of letting go is to be willing to feel your hurt. This is important because it's the automatic avoidance of this hurt that forces us to resist.

We think that we're resisting our circumstances but we're not. We are resisting all the feelings and emotion that are being reactivated by our circumstances.

More accurately, we are resisting a very specific hurt from the past. We are resisting the hurt of feeling not good enough, worthless, not worth loving, or some other form of being not okay.

Once you find and heal this hurt, the need to resist or hang on disappears. You can then let go and take the action you need to effectively handle your situation. Finding and healing this hurt is one of the most important things you can ever do.

This hurt is responsible for all your fear and all your upsets. It is responsible for all your self-sabotaging behavior patterns and ultimately, all of your suffering.

Courtesy: Bill Fergusson, masteryoflife.com

Practical Suggestion No.

2

EXPECT THE BEST AND GET IT

If you study the habits of happy, contented, successful people, you will realise they know exactly how to respond to circumstances, positive or negative as they may be. They know exactly what they must do under any given circumstances – or, if they don't, they master and perfect the technique over a period of time; for I believe that successful people are also 'learning' people: they are lifelong learners in the school of experience. They know when they have to push really hard; they know when they have to take initiatives; they know when it is time to take risks; they know when they must stand still and not rock the boat; they know when they have to keep on plodding, no matter how unrewarding it may seem; and of course, they know when to let go, and let God take over the problems they cannot solve.

Successful people are always positive and optimistic in their outlook. Their attitude to the proverbial half glass is to regard it as half-full, not half-empty!

Optimism is defined as "an inclination to put the most favourable construction upon actions and events or to anticipate their best possible outcome". It is thought to be the philosophical opposite of pessimism. Pessimism, derived from the Latin root, *pessimus* (worst), is a state of mind which makes our perception of life negative, especially with regard to future events. Optimists generally believe that people and events are inherently good, so that most situations work out in the end for the best. Pessimism, on the other hand, is sometimes thought to be a negative self-fulfilling prophecy; that if an individual feels that something is bad, it is likely to get worse! Oscar Wilde defined a Pessimist thus: "One who, when he has the choice of two evils, chooses both."

No man, no situation or circumstance can harm us if we have a positive attitude. For, a positive attitude is self-friendly and hence, it will never let you down. As Harry Truman once said, "A pessimist is one who makes difficulties of his opportunities and an optimist is one who makes opportunities of his difficulties."

Today, scientists are beginning to understand the value and power of what is called 'thought energy'. They are beginning to study what our ancient *rishis* knew thousands of years ago. I am indeed happy that this truth has been reaffirmed in our days by influential thinkers and scientists. One of the fundamental laws of life is: "Energy follows thought." As we think, so we become. If we fear a fall, we fall down. To put it simply, we are what we think. Hence we should be very careful with our thoughts.

Thoughts have an inherent capacity to materialise. When you expect the best, you are likely to get it; when you expect the worst, the worst is likely to happen!

When your mind is filled with negative emotions, you become insecure and fearful. You are overcome by negative thought patterns; "I may fail," or "I may loose my money," or "People may laugh at me," and so on.

This kind of thinking weighs you down. You let opportunities and chances slip by; you are afraid to make bold moves; you begin to stagnate…

As you think, so you become, is the immutable law of nature. Fill your mind with thoughts of joy, love, peace and harmony; these aspects will be reflected in your life. Give way to fear and despair – you will sink into abject misery.

Pessimism, the negative way of looking at life, is a thoroughly destructive attitude. It is the greatest joy-killer. It not only blights one's life, it is also an infectious disease which its 'carriers' transmit to others.

All of us would love to be clairvoyants and know exactly how things are going to turn out for us – at work, in our relationships, in our examinations and in every other aspect of our lives. Wouldn't we give anything to have that legendary crystal ball into which we could all gaze and find out all about the future! But God, in His infinite wisdom has chosen to keep the future hidden from us. So what do we do? We can expect the best and hope that things will turn out well. Or, we can expect the worst and conclude that things are going to turn out badly.

If we have had a few bad experiences in life – been betrayed, let down, or disappointed, we are often reluctant to hope for the best.

At first glance, this would seem the sensible stance to take. If you expect the worst, and it doesn't happen, surely that is good? And if the worst actually does happen, you will at least have the satisfaction of being right, of knowing it all beforehand. And indeed, this is the argument put forward by many pessimists to justify their position. However, contrary to what you might expect, the facts do not bear out the 'being better off for that' part of the argument.

But research carried out by Professor Richard Wiseman, a psychologist at the University of Hertfordshire, has uncovered the real explanation why 'lucky' people (who naturally expect the best), get more out of life, and 'unlucky' people (who naturally expect the worst) have such a hard time of it.

Wiseman discovered that 'lucky' people generate their own good fortune via four basic principles:

- they are skilled at creating and noticing chance opportunities
- they make lucky decisions by listening to their intuition
- they create self-fulfilling prophesies via positive expectations
- they adopt a resilient attitude to life that transforms bad luck into good.

Wiseman's fascinating research showed that pessimistic people, who expected things not to go well for them, consistently miss positive opportunities, even when these are put in front of them in the most dramatic way possible. It is as if they become 'blind' to opportunities.

It is said that John Ruskin had a carved stone on his desk, used as a paper-weight; engraved on it was a single word: *Today*.

Live today; live in the present; live *now* – you cannot wait indefinitely for an ideal tomorrow which may or may not come.

"Too many of us wait for the perfect circumstances," said a learned man, "with the result that we do nothing, achieve nothing." Get on with your life; go ahead; start *now* ! Regrets over the past or the dread of the future are futile; if we are obsessed with them, we will have nothing to show for all the decades we have lived.

Researchers from the Mayo Clinic interviewed over 800 people to assess and rate their optimism levels, then tracked them for 35 years to see how long they lived. They found that regardless of age or sex, the optimists lived longer. The pessimists died prematurely. In fact, for every 10 percent increase in the pessimism index, there were 20 percent more early deaths.

Edward L. Schneider, a writer and researcher on longevity, tells us that happy people are healthier and out-survive their pessimistic or depressed counterparts. Optimism is associated with feelings of better health, more vitality, higher mental health ratings, and lower levels of pain. Depression has the opposite effect. Feeling good is not a luxury; it's a basic component of health. "Engaging the world with an expectation of the best can give you a longer, better life," he concludes.

Optimistic people aim high; they never underestimate themselves; they never allow themselves to under-perform.

A distinguished statesman was visiting a forest that had been devastated by fire. After taking a tally of the trees that had been destroyed, he declared, "We must replant the cedars."

"They take two thousand years to grow to their full height!" someone remarked.

"Two thousand years?" said the statesman. "In that case, my friend, there's not a minute to lose. Let's start on the replantation drive immediately."

In a research on working women, it was found that even among those doing the same kind of jobs, some people viewed work as a series of hassles, while others saw it as a positive experience in which they were in control of their lives. Among those who felt positive about their work, satisfaction was 30% higher.

If you would see your work only as a 'job' then it drags you down. If you see it as a calling, a vocation, then it is no longer toil or trouble. It becomes an expression of your self, a part of you.

A distinguished visitor arrived at a quarry where several poor labourers were toiling hard. He went up to a few of them and asked just one question of each man: "What are you doing?"

The first one snarled angrily, "Can't you see I am breaking stones?"

The second one wiped the sweat off his brow and replied, "I am earning a living to feed my wife and children."

The third man looked up at him and said cheerfully, "I am helping to build a beautiful temple!"

You can imagine which of these men got the most out of his work.

Whether you are at home, or in the workplace or among friends, you must exude optimism and positive thinking – and you will find it reflected right back at you!

If you are facing a challenge – trying to win a game or just finish a difficult assignment, what kind of people would you like to have with you? Pessimistic people who keep telling you that you will fail – or positive people who motivate you to expect the best?

We always gravitate towards optimists who expect the best out of life. Living a happy, contented life is a great challenge – and a great achievement. It is a challenge that is best met with optimism.

"I am overwhelmed by constant anxiety," a sister said to me.

"What is it that you worry about?" I asked her.

"I'm worried about my daughter, who is expecting a baby," she began. "Also, I'm anxious to find a suitable girl for my only son."

"If that is your..." I began.

"That's not all," she interrupted. "I have only just begun."

"Do go on," I sighed.

"I'm worried about my husband's blood pressure," she continued. "And I'm constantly anxious about my old mother who lives all alone in the village. And I'm on edge at my workplace. I don't think my boss appreciates my work. And I'm dreadfully worried about the future! What will become of our savings with inflation rising so high, and interest rates falling constantly..."

I was reminded of the words of Seneca: "He grieves more than is necessary, who grieves *before* it is necessary."

Many people complain of stress, tension and nervous exhaustion. I am inclined to think that this is seldom the result of present trouble or work, but of trouble or work *anticipated.* It comes with the constant strain of looking ahead and climbing mountains before we ever reach the foothills.

"I'm so unhappy and worried this morning," one woman complained to another.

"What is it?" asked her friend sympathetically.

"I was worrying about something last night," said the woman, "and now I can't, for the life of me, remember what it was."

It is said that the first experimental steam engines actually wasted ninety percent of the energy of the coal they used. When the electric dynamo was designed, it was said to utilise ninety percent of the power, with the wastage just reduced to ten percent. When we worry constantly, we too, fritter away all our energy in fretting, fuming, in scolding and complaining.

It is in *our* hands to convert all our energy into power, vitality and the sunshine of good cheer!

What about real, financial problems, you may ask. What about businessmen who face failure and loss?

Yes, you have to face these problems head on – but you must take them on with a clear head, not one that is clouded and flustered with worry. Besides, worry is useless in such circumstance, and cannot really correct the problem. So why waste time worrying?

Of Guru Amardas, we are told that every evening, he gave away all that he had, keeping not a grain of corn for the morrow, not even a copper coin in his purse. Before night fell, he emptied his store of provisions – even drained the pitchers dry!

"The morrow will take care of itself!" he said to his disciples who were amazed by his strange behaviour. And the morrow did take care of itself!

"Ah," you might say, "the Guru was an ascetic. It is easy for the likes of him to live from day to day..."

Let me tell you, the Guru was a family man with wife and children. Each and everyday, he held a *langar* (fellowship meal) at which many pilgrims and passers by ate their fill. He ran a common kitchen which cooked food for them all! But his faith in the Lord was unshakable. And the Lord never failed him.

Let me remind you of that beautiful passage in the Bible where Jesus exhorts us to walk with God today and trust Him for the morrow.

Once, pointing to a procession of ants, he said to his disciples, "Ye of little faith! Look at the ants: who gives them their daily food?"

And one of the disciples said, "Master, they need so little!"

"Then look at the birds," said Jesus. "They toil not, nor do they save for the morrow. Yet they get their daily food and are happy!"

And the disciple said, "Master, birds have wings with which they fly and pluck fruits from trees!"

"And what about the wild beasts?" Jesus asked. "How fat they are! They have no wings. Yet they too, get their daily food!"

When you feel that He is taking care of your needs, you cease to worry! You do not have to plan in advance for unforeseen eventualities. You do not have to worry about calamities. You simply allow the Divine Plan to unfold. You claim nothing; you ask nothing; you seek nothing; you plan nothing. You simply become a channel for the Divine Plan to flow through.

How many of us are capable of such faith and trust?

Think about it...

Jeff Cohen, the founder of solveyourproblems.com emphasises what he calls 'the law of attraction' to ensure that we expect the best and get it. Here are his simple suggestions to cultivate powerful expectations backed up with firm conviction and unwavering faith:

1. First, you must choose to expect the best in every situation. This will be challenging if you don't have full control of your thoughts yet. If you haven't developed a strong focus, you'll probably keep vacillating back and forth between random thoughts and focused thoughts until you train your mind. Simply keep at it! Keep saying things like, "I know this is going to work out for the best," or "I know I will turn this situation to my advantage somehow," or "I expect the best and the best always comes to me!"

2. Avoid negative talk like the plague. By "negative talk" I mean complaining, arguing, or doom predictions – anything that drags down your emotions and contradicts your positive expectations. If other people try to engage you in negative talk, you may have to be firm to avoid it. You might also need to limit the amount of time you spend with negative people. Try to always phrase your statements in a positive way. Instead of saying, "This won't be easy," say, "I can handle this."

3. KNOW that your expectation will come true. You may wonder how to "know" when you really don't know yet! If it hasn't happened yet, how can you be sure it will? This type of knowing is based solely on

faith. You are CHOOSING to know. It might take awhile to get comfortable with this, but once you do it becomes a lot easier. In order to really know, you're going to have to completely banish doubt and disbelief from your mind. When they pop up, simply push them out of your mind and affirm again that you KNOW your expectation will happen.

These three simple things can make a world of difference in your ability to attract what you want, and when the actualisations start showing up in your life, you'll be able to add that much more faith and confidence to your expectations – which will make them still more effective!

Courtesy: solveyourproblems.com

Practical Suggestion No.

3

KEEP MOVING!

Whatever be the circumstances in which you are placed, whatever the conditions around you, keep moving! Get on with your work! Leave the rest to God!

May I tell you, I learnt this lesson from an ant which I came across on the seashore, a long time ago. I was relaxing on the beach, when I saw this tiny ant hurrying past me. My attention was on the majestic rolling waves at that time; but this tiny creature, scurrying about on the sand, caught my attention. In a playful mood, I decided to get to know this ant better. I made a tiny little heap of sand on its path – I say 'tiny little heap' from our human perspective; for the ant, it must have been a little hillock! I created this little hill on the ant's path. But she quietly came to the base of the hillock, climbed up the slope, climbed down the other side and went on her way. Now I created a valley, that is, dug a deep trench on her path. Quietly, she went down the trench, crossed it and continued her journey. Not one to give up my experiment,

I placed a large pebble on her path. She reached the stone, considered climbing it, realised that she could not; she struggled for a while, fell down a couple of times; she stopped a while to reconsider the situation, and then took the longer route around the stone and moved on! My next obstacle for her was a long twig. She saw the twig, struggled with it, found a way around and kept moving!

Keep moving! Whatever be the problem, whatever be the obstacles on your path, keep moving! Not once did my ant allow herself to 'get stuck' as we put it. Not once did she call upon her companions for help – and I am convinced quite a few of them were available in the vicinity. She just kept moving on!

Keep moving on! Keep moving on and the potential that is within you will be unfolded. The tremendous *shakti* within you will be released.

Sri Krishna tells us in the Bhagavad Gita of the man who is the ideal doer, the *saatvic karta*:

> The doer who is free from attachment, whose speech is devoid of egotism, who is full of resolution and zeal, and who is unchanged by success or failure, he is called *saatvic karta* (the pure or rightful doer).
>
> **(XVIII-26)**

Now I can hear some of you murmuring in protest, "But Dada, we live and work on the worldly plane, where we have to be concerned about the fruits of our action! How can you equate us with Arjuna?"

I am well aware that you must fulfill your business concerns and your profit motives. But my point is this; while you are working, while you are implementing your strategy to succeed, any thought of profit must be a source of distraction for you. Even management pundits would say to you, that your focus in the crucial strategy must be on planning and execution, not on the party you will throw when you have succeeded! And believe me, the Gita has taught your management experts a lot of valuable insights!

So, keep moving!

Many a time, we are overawed by the impediments and delays and the thousand-and-one hurdles that seem to be specially brought out on our path, even in routine everyday activities. I understand that for certain categories of salary earners in India, the Income Tax Department has now brought out a special form called *Saral* (meaning, easy and simple). But many people still remember the complicated returns that people were expected to fill out twenty or thirty years ago! Only a qualified chartered accountant could understand the small print and fill in all those details and the innumerable calculations and sub totals that had to be filled even for a salary of Rs. 10,000 in those days! Friends have assured me that they were literally 'tearing their hair' by the time the forms could be filled.

Things have improved considerably, I am told, as far as the IT returns are concerned. But other routine requirements, still present insurmountable obstacles. Going to the *zilla parishad* for a domicile certificate; applying to the RTO for a license renewal; getting an NOC for a construction – such tasks require tremendous reserves of patience and determination. Each and every table, each and every attendant and clerk in the government offices, seem to be placed where they are for the express purpose of hampering any progress you wish to make!

And these are just routine applications. Think of tougher tasks like applying for a housing loan or a business loan; think of applications made to foreign universities; think of setting up your own business; think of working for your Ph.D.; think of shifting premises; think of executing a complex project successfully; think of working with a team to achieve a goal. In all of these endeavours, we celebrate success in a spectacular way, when the desired result is achieved. But who can forget the tough grind, the slow progress, the frustrating delays and the near desperate conditions that we had to cross before success was assured? And the one thing that assured success was this – that we kept moving, that we did not give up, no matter what the provocation!

On a cold winter's day, with the temperature below zero, an old pilgrim was making his way to a shrine on the Himalayas.

"My dear sir," exclaimed a young fellow traveller who was passing by, "how will you ever reach the shrine, on your own, in such a cold season?"

"My heart got there first," replied the old man cheerfully. "It's easy for the rest of me to follow!"

Within each and every one of us is a tremendous potential to overcome obstacles and achieve success; to face difficulties and overcome them. There is just one thing we have to do to tap this vast potential, this tremendous power, we must believe in ourselves, and we must keep moving.

The Chinese proverb tells us, does it not, that even the journey of a thousand miles begins with one first step? So let's take one step at a time; let's keep moving towards our goal.

I said, let's keep moving towards our goal, our desired destination; for when I insist on moving, I do not mean drifting aimlessly. Several years ago, a cartoon appeared in an American newspaper. It showed aliens, the inhabitants of Mars looking at people on earth. One martian asks another, "What are those people doing on earth?" The other replies, "They are moving." "Where are they moving?" persists the first one. "They do not know where they are moving. They are just moving," is the reply.

That is not the kind of movement I meant!

So many of us today, are just drifting through life. We do not know where we are going; we do not even know what we want out of life. We work like machines, going through the same routine day after day. We forget that each of us is unique. They say that there are hundred million people in India today. Just imagine, among those hundred million people there is no one exactly like you! Why, amongst the billions of people, who inhabit the earth, there is no other person who is like you!

You are unique. God made you for a special purpose. Discover that special purpose. Make it your goal and once you have fixed that goal, you must keep your eyes fixed always on that goal. You must keep moving steadily towards that goal.

If I were to ask you right now: "What is that you want out of life? What do you wish to achieve?" Not many of you will be able to give me an answer straight away. But if I were to phrase the same question in a negative manner, "What is it that you feel you cannot achieve?" many of you will have ready answers. Some of you will say to me, "Achievement does not run in our family. My father achieved nothing; my brother achieved nothing. I shall achieve nothing." Perhaps others will say, "I do not have the power, the education or the influence and the resources to achieve whatever I want" Yet others might say, "My brother has all the brains in the family and my sister has all the good looks, I have nothing, so I cannot do anything." To each of you I would say, you must fix your goal. It may be a material goal or a spiritual goal - but you must fix your goal, and everyday, you must move forward, you must do everything in your power to reach that goal!

We are just moving; we are just drifting. But if we wish to succeed, we must fix our goal and move towards the goal! We should be able to describe our goal vividly. We should fix it in our imagination. And we should have an unswerving focus on the goal all the time. We must keep moving towards the goal, one step at a time, one day at a time!

I am sure all of you have heard the name of Jesse Owens, the black American who won three Olympic gold medals and created a record at the Munich games. Jesse was born with scrawny legs – lean, weak, bony legs. But one day, the man who was known in those days as the fastest runner in the world, Charlie Paddock, came to his school. Addressing the boys, Paddock said, "You can be what you want to be in life. Decide what you want to be, then go to God and ask Him to help you to become what you want to be."

These words penetrated young Jesse's consciousness. After the lecture, he went up on the dais to meet Charlie Paddock and said to him, "Will you shake hands with me?" Paddock smiled and shook hands with him, and Jesse felt as if an electric current had passed through his entire being. He went out to the playground and started jumping. He kept on jumping, and in this upbeat mood, he met the sports coach and said to him, "I have a dream! I have a dream!" The coach asked him, "My boy, what is your dream?" Jesse Owens, the boy with the scrawny legs, replied, "I want to be the fastest man alive – like Charlie Paddock!"

The coach patted the boy on the shoulder and said to him, "It is good to have a dream, but you have to take steps to fulfill your dream. You must build a ladder to reach the dream!"

What is the ladder that one must build to reach one's dream? This ladder is made up of four rungs – the four rungs are determination, dedication, discipline and a positive attitude.

Jesse Owen built this ladder, and he began to keep on moving towards his dream, one step at a time, one rung at a time; and the dream he cherished came true one day. Jesse entered the Olympic Games. He ran the 100 meters, and won gold; he ran the 400 meters, and won gold; as for high jump, he not only won gold, but created an Olympic record that remained unbeaten for several years to come!

Just imagine, a weak boy with scrawny legs set a goal for himself, and achieved it! And yet we complain, "I don't have the strength... I don't have the resources... I don't have the influence to achieve what I want!"

Fix a goal and keep an unwavering focus on it all the time! Keep on moving towards your goal with determination, discipline, dedication and a positive attitude!

When Abraham Lincoln was a young boy, he husked corn for three days so that he could earn a little money, to pay for a second hand copy of *The Life Of Washington*. He read the book avidly, and said to a woman he knew – Mrs. Crawford by name: "I don't always intend to do this you know - delve, grub, husk corn, split rails and the like."

"What do you want to be then?" asked Mrs. Crawford. "I shall be the President," announced Abraham Lincoln. "I shall study and get ready and the chance will come."

The chance came and Abraham was ready to take on the most powerful position in the land – for he had fixed his goal early, and kept moving towards it steadily!

It has been said that winners make goals, while losers make excuses!

If you wish to succeed in life you must prepare a plan. Everyday, as you get up in the morning, you must plan on what you wish to do that day. Remember, time is the most precious of all possessions and we waste our precious time in idle pursuits, doing nothing.

Planning for today goes with yet another vital precept: take one step at a time; live one day at a time! So many of us are overwhelmed by the work we have to do. "There's so much work to be done," we groan. "I can't take it any more. It's too much for me to handle!" We blame ourselves for not doing enough yesterday, we think of all that we can postpone to tomorrow, with the result that we do not concentrate on what we have to do today. There is an old saying which tells us, "When you have one eye fixed on yesterday and another eye fixed on tomorrow, you are sure to be cross-eyed today."

Every one of us is given the same number of hours everyday. Rich people cannot buy more hours. Scientist cannot invent more minutes. Clever people cannot stretch time. Misers cannot save time to hoard it and spend it another day. And yet, it has been pointed out, time is always fair and forgiving. No matter how much time you have wasted in the past, you have a full day before you every morning. Your success depends on your using it wisely and well – by planning and setting priorities.

The wise have always emphasised that an intelligent plan is a vital step to success. The man who plans well knows where he is going, knows what progress he is making, and has a pretty good idea when he will arrive!

There was an old woman who had an issue to sort out with the welfare department which took care of her pension. For the last few weeks, her pension was getting credited after a great delay; the local post office had advised her to go to the welfare office in the city to lodge a complaint, as the delay was due to a computer error.

The lady was overwhelmed by the sheer size of the office and the hundreds of people who worked there and the thousands who seemed to be standing in queues here and there before counters and windows. With great difficulty, she managed to locate the tiny office on the twelfth floor which handled pension funds and related complaints.

Nervously, she stepped inside to find a young woman seated at a table listening to an old man who had a long story to narrate about his problem. She listened to the old man patiently, noted the details of his complaint, helped him fill a form, and having reassured him that his problem would be sorted out, sent him off with a cheerful goodbye.

Six other people were seated in the tiny room, and each one took their place at the table to narrate their story of woe. The young woman listened to each one with the same unfailing courtesy and patience. Never once did she lose her cool; never once did she raise her voice; never once did she show so much as a trace of irritation. Each and every person who took up at least ten minutes of her time were sent off satisfied and reassured.

At long last it was the old lady's turn. She had been watching the young woman spellbound, listening to every word uttered across the table. As soon as she took her seat, she could not help blurting out, "My dear, how do you do it? How can you be so sweet and understanding with old people like me? And how many people like me do you handle everyday?"

The young woman smiled. "Only one at a time!" she said cheerfully. "Why should I keep count when I have only one person sitting across the table from me? And when I'm talking to you, you are the focus of all my attention. I do not look at how many went before you, or how many are waiting to come after you. And I find that I can give my best to nice people like you when I look at them individually! And believe me, the time flies when I take an interest in what you have to say. My goal is to send each one away with the reassurance that their problem will be solved. I am so happy to see that their minds are at peace when they leave the table. It is so wonderful to know that they are ready to trust me with their problems. Do you know how many good friends I have made across this table?"

So, keep moving! When you have set a goal before you, when you have set out to accomplish something, you must never, never, never give it up. If you are sure that you have chosen the right goal, if you are confident that it is the right thing to do, that it will not hurt or harm anyone – keep moving towards your goal.

Patience is not a passive virtue, as some people think. Patience, as experts are now beginning to understand, is a 'proactive choice' and a vital way of perseverance that keeps you moving towards your goal.

Think about it...

Nicolo Paganini was a well-known and gifted nineteenth century violinist. He was also well known as a great showman with a quick sense of humor. His most memorable concert was in Italy with a full orchestra. He was performing before a packed house and his technique was incredible, his tone was fantastic, and his audience dearly loved him. Toward the end of his concert, Paganini was astounding his audience with an unbelievable composition when suddenly one string on his violin snapped and hung limply from his instrument. Paganini frowned briefly, shook his head, and continued to play, improvising beautifully.

Then to everyone's surprise, a second string broke. And shortly thereafter, a third. Almost like a slapstick comedy, Paganini stood there with three strings dangling from his Stradivarius. But instead of leaving the stage, Paganini stood his ground and calmly completed the difficult number on the one remaining string.

You may be sure he received the standing ovation that he so richly deserved!

If we are facing in the right direction, all we have to do is keep on walking.

–Buddhist Saying

Practical Suggestion No.

4

CONQUER FEAR

The famous essayist Montaigne once confessed: "The thing I fear most is fear."

Fear casts its dark shadow over our lives at one time or another. We are prone to fear almost instinctively. Neither the highest nor the lowest of us is exempt from fear. The most powerful nations fear their rivals and neighbours. Politicians are afraid of losing elections. Students are afraid of failing in examinations. Mothers are afraid about their children's safety... the list is endless.

Fear is the one mark that characterises us, children of a skeptical age. We are afraid of the future, afraid of poverty, afraid of unemployment, afraid of dishonour and disgrace, afraid of disease and death – it seems to me that sometimes, we are afraid of life itself!

We live in fear; we work in fear; we walk in fear; we talk in fear. We move through life from one fear to another, crushed beneath the weight of a woeful existence!

Fear is at the root of all our problems. Fear is the starting point for all evil. Fear gives rise to all our misfortune. Living in constant fear saps our vital energies, leaving us too drained and exhausted to savour the joy of life. Fear paralyses the mind, even as a stroke paralyses the body. It strikes at the nervous system; it causes stress and tension. It undermines our well-being. Worst of all, it robs us of happiness and destroys our peace of mind.

It was Marie Curie who said: "Nothing in life is to be feared; it is only to be understood."

When Swami Vivekananda returned from America and entered upon his work of regeneration in India, the one message which he delivered to the people as he travelled from town to town, from village to village, in this ancient land of heroes and sages was this: "Be bold! Be fearless!"

Anyone who reads Swamiji's words is sure to feel a thrill, a sense of power – even today! Here are a few words which I love to recall: "Stand up, be bold, be strong! Strength is life, weakness is death. Weakness is the one cause of suffering. We become miserable because we are weak. We lie, steal, kill and commit other crimes, because we are weak. We suffer, because we are weak. Where there is nothing to weaken us, there is no death, no sorrow."

"The mind is its own place," wrote Milton, "and in itself, can create a heaven of Hell, a Hell of Heaven." How true! The mind can create fears and phobias; it can also create security and self-confidence. If we are to live a life of joy, harmony and freedom from fear, we must be fearless in the mind within.

Do you wish to overcome your fears and phobias? There are two options open to you. One is to submit to your fears, allow yourself to be overwhelmed by them, making your life miserable in the process. I'm afraid very many people adopt this course. They live with their fear and all their lives, suffering needless misery and anxiety. What a great pity this!

The other option – the wiser alternative – is to conquer your fears, with God's help. When you do this, you achieve a remarkable victory that can change your life. This victory is not the prerogative of the holy, the mighty and the brave. All of us have the potential to achieve it.

How can you free yourself from the clutches of fear? The first step is to become aware that fear, like all other human weaknesses, is removable. It was not put into you by God. You acquired it somewhere along the way: you took it on yourself, or it was put into you by the environment in which you live. Whatever it was, *fear is removable.*

Are you prone to anger and irritation? These can be removed. Are you given to bouts of depression and despair? These are removable. Do you suffer from inferiority complex? It is also removable!

The important thing is for you to realise that you are not condemned to live with fear all your life. It is removable! Once you realise this fact, you can begin to work on the process of actually removing it. This is possible through faith in God and self-discipline.

People are anxious when the budget is presented in Parliament. People worry when OPEC countries raise oil prices. People are afraid when foreigners come to live in their locality. People worry when share prices fall. Anything and everything triggers fear these days!

The 'logic' of fear is truly illogical. We are afraid of losing our jobs – but we are afraid to go out and seek new positions. I know some people who are terrified of contracting a major illness – but they are even more scared to meet a specialist and go through a series of tests. Some young women are afraid of marriage, as they feel that they would lose their identity – but the idea of remaining single makes them feel insecure! There are very many old people who are terrified of the long, lonely years that lie ahead of them – but they are haunted by the fear of death!

As I said, we are afraid to die – and we are afraid to live, because life had become so complicated, risky and insecure!

"A ship in the harbour is safe," goes the saying. But that is not what ships are built for!

Life demands of us that we live with courage. Winston Churchill considered courage to be the greatest of all virtues – because we cannot exhibit any other virtue without it. Without the courage to act, justice would be impossible. Without the courage to love, compassion and understanding would not exist. Without the courage to endure, faith and hope would not flourish!

Linguistic experts relate the English word *courage* to the French word *Coeur*, meaning heart. Courage is born of the heart. It is the heart's response to the impulse of fear.

The Bhagavad Gita tells us

> Meet the transient world
> With neither grasping nor fear,
> Trust the unfolding of life
> And you will attain true serenity.

The uncertainties of life have to be taken on, in the spirit of acceptance. Escape and running away are no solutions. It was Helen Keller who said:

> Security is mostly a superstition. It does not exist in nature, nor do children as a whole experience it. Avoiding danger is no safer in the long run than outright exposure. Life is either a daring adventure or nothing.

A business executive was flying long distance across the Pacific. A little boy travelling home for his holidays, was seated next to him. As the passengers were dozing after an excellent lunch, there was an urgent message from the pilot to fasten their seat-belts, as the plane was about to run into stormy weather, heavy rain and wind. Despite the enormous size of the plane and the power of its engines, the flight was jolted badly.

The boy became desperately afraid and clung to the older man's arms. For his part, the man stroked the boy's head gently to reassure him.

"Aren't you afraid?" whispered the boy, as the plane dipped all of a sudden.

"No!" laughed the man. "This is real fun, isn't it? Aren't you enjoying yourself?"

An immediate change came over the little boy. His fear and tension left him and he too, began to enjoy the "fun" laughing and squealing delightedly as the plane dipped and swayed.

The executive had taught the young one a valuable lesson in the art of living!

"Cowards die many deaths," goes the proverb. "The brave die but once." True it is that each of us has only one life – but how many of us 'die a thousand deaths' in fear and nervousness!

Freedom from fear is achieved through perseverance, tenacity and sheer will power. Have you heard about the teacher who asked the smartest boy in class, "Tell me Hari, what is the difference between perseverance and obstinacy?"

The clever lad replied, "One is a strong will, and the other is a strong won't."

Only they can conquer fear, who have willed themselves to do so!

We must never underestimate mind-power, the power of the will. Freedom from fear – as well as health, happiness and harmony – depend in thought-habits. Truly has it been said that even happiness is the product of habitual right-thinking.

Try and imagine a huge slab of ice one-and-a-half miles square, and 92 millions miles high. It would reach from the earth to the sun.

Scientists tell us that this gigantic cake of ice would be completely melted in 30 seconds – if the full power of the sun were focussed upon it.

Mental sunshine is equally powerful! When you have the will to be free of fear, the sunshine of your faith and confidence will melt the ice of insecurity and dread. Mental sunshine will cause the flowers of peace and joy and serenity to bloom wherever you go!

Therefore, cultivate the will to be unafraid – create your own mental sunshine!

For your reflection...

Five Steps to Unleashing Your Power Over Fear

1. Become "ignorant" to fear:

Fear appears in many different forms. It can come from negative self (i.e. "I can't do this," "I'm not good at this," etc.). It can come from negative media forecasts (i.e. bad predictions of the economy, bad weather reports, reports of murder, rape, etc.). Therefore, you must mute the voice of fear by limiting (or completely eliminating) your contact with fear-causing entities (i.e. news reports, newspapers, failure-conscious people, etc.).

2. Don't let fear have time to think:

Thoughts are powerful. A single thought can be responsible for life or death in this world. And anything that you think about long enough will find its way into the physical realm. Therefore, if you were to spend time thinking about the things that you want out of life (I mean conscious concentration), you begin to see them. Conversely, the same is true for the things that you don't want in life. Commit your time to faith and believing, not fear and doubt.

3. Always speak with faith and belief:

According to the scriptures, life and death are in the power of the tongue. God framed this world from faithful speech (Genesis 1). Fear lives in doubt and disbelief. To frame your own world free of debilitating fear, always think, act, and speak positively in faith and belief. Be bold and say things as you want them to be in your life. If it is a new house you want, say it! If it is a new car you want, say it! If it is a successful family life you want, say it! If it is a better job that you want, say it! As Henry Ford once stated, "Whether you think you can or you can't, you're right."

4. Create and maintain a positive outlook of yourself:

I have a motto that goes like this, "If I know who and what I am, no one can tell me who and what I am not!" No matter what the world has decided to think about me, I have decided to think great thoughts about myself. Therefore, I am free of world's often limiting belief system. I don't worry about things like weather reports, poor economic forecasts, what celebrity just went to jail, and who does not believe in my dreams, because if God is for me, who or what can be against me (Romans 8:31)? Decide who and what you are right now and do not be moved by negativity.

5. Continue to execute the thing(s) that you fear until fear disappears:

Success is active. Action dispels fear. If you sit still, fear has the time to paralyse your abilities and efforts, ultimately, causing you to fail. Continue to move toward your goals with great diligence and great courage!

Courtesy: Myles W. Miller

Practical Suggestion No. 5

THINK OF SOLUTIONS – NOT PROBLEMS

Let me begin this chapter with a lovely Swedish legend. It tells us that God before He sends His children to this earth, gives each one of us a carefully selected and packaged gift – a set of problems. He promises us with His Divine smile, that each package is unique and meant exclusively for us. Each set of problems, He explains, carries with it a set of unique blessings, meant for our special benefit. No one else may have the blessings these problems will bring to us. And along with these problems, He also gives us those special talents and unique abilities that will be needed to make these problems our servants.

"Now go down to your birth and to your forgetfulness of the past," He tells us. "Know that I love you beyond measure. These problems that I give you are a symbol of that love. The success you make of your life with the help of your problems will be a symbol of your love for Me, your Heavenly Father."

It was a wise man who said: "When problems surface, insights disappear; when insights surface, problems disappear. Problems and insights rarely make a joint appearance."

One of the major causes of killer diseases like hypertension and stress is that we are overwhelmed by the problems we face. I always say that problems are wonderful presents that are thrown at us by Providence – only, we fail to recognise the gift because it comes wrapped up in a soiled package. The word 'problem' is derived from the Latin word "*pro balo*" and means that which is deliberately thrown in our way. It is because we react to problems negatively that we create panic and stress within ourselves.

It has been said that a problem is like a pebble. If you hold it close to your eye, it seems magnified, and it blocks your entire vision. If you hold it at an arms length, you can see its shape, its colour and its size. If you drop it at your feet, you can effortlessly walk over it!

If you wish to find solutions to your problems, there is a basic rule you must follow: always be positive in your approach and attitude to life.

When the well-known preacher and writer of inspirational books, Norman Vincent Peale, was a young man, he had a very difficult time coping with a few tough problems that had cropped up in his life. He took his problems to an older, trusted friend, to whom he complained, "Why can't I cope with these problems?"

The friend reflected for a while and then suggested, "Maybe it's because you are not grateful enough."

Peale was perplexed. What did he mean by 'not grateful enough'?

The older man explained about what he held to be the law of life: focus on your troubles and they will multiply; count your blessings, and your life will grow more and more joyous.

"My advice to you Norman," he concluded, "is that you become less of a complainer and more of a thanksgiver. I assure you that you will be able to manage all your problems."

Peale found that this advice really worked. "In some unfathomable way," he writes, "the acknowledgement of past blessings seems to be the activation of new blessings."

There are people who focus their attention only on problems and difficulties. Tell them of your dreams and plans, and they will say, "No, No! It is impossible! It will never work." They will point out all the drawbacks and weakness in your plan, and try their best to convince you that you cannot win. These are the people who can boast, "Bring me a solution and I will give you a problem!"

The truth is, there is no problem that does not have a solution. The man with the positive attitude thinks of the solution – while the man with the negative attitude only thinks of the problem. We need people who bring solutions to problems, not problems to solutions.

Be positive in your approach and you will find solutions to all your problems. The man with the positive attitude may be surrounded by adverse conditions, but he will look for a place to stand on; he will seek a solution; he will expect the best results; and he will invariably succeed. Remember, this is the great law of life. That, which you expect, always comes to you. Therefore, why not expect the very best? Expect success and you will achieve success!

It is said that Alexander Kuzmin, mayor of the city of Megion in western Siberia, told his officials that they must stop using phrases such as "I don't know" and "It's lunch time" when citizens approached them with problems. Mr. Kuzmin felt that city officials should help improve people's lives and solve their problems, not make excuses!

"Bring me solutions, not problems" is a phrase that former British Prime Minister Margaret Thatcher was well known for using.

A friend said to me the other day that there is actually a website called "Solutions, not problems" operated by a consultancy service provider!

One of the most memorable case studies on Japanese management was the case of the empty soap carton, which happened in one of Japan's biggest cosmetics companies. The company received a complaint that a consumer had bought a premium brand of soap and found the box was empty. Immediately the authorities isolated the problem to the assembly line, which transported all the packaged boxes of soap to the delivery department. For some reason, one soap box went through the assembly line empty. Management asked its engineers to solve the problem.

Highly qualified engineers worked hard to devise an X-ray machine with high-resolution monitors which would be manned by two people to watch all the soap boxes that passed through the line to ensure they were not empty.

No doubt, they worked hard and they worked fast but they spent an astronomical amount to do so.

But when an ordinary assembly-line worker in a small company was posed with the same problem, he did not get into such complications as X-ray machines and monitors; he came out with a simpler solution. He bought a strong industrial electric fan and pointed it at the assembly line. He switched the fan on, and as each soap box passed the fan, it simply blew the empty boxes out of the line.

We would do well to remember that not all problems require complicated solutions; in fact, some solutions are really simple ... so let us learn to focus on solutions, not on problems!

David W. Hartman of Pennsylvania became blind when he was eight years old. He had always dreamt of studying medicine; but the medical school to which he applied for admission discouraged him severely by pointing out that no one with visual disability had ever completed a medical course. Hartman refused to be negative. Courageously, he took on the task of "reading" by having twenty-five medical textbooks audio recorded for him. At twenty-seven, David W. Hartman became the first blind student to complete medical school.

There were two men who came to a Rehabilitation Center for the disabled. Each one of them had lost an arm.

At the end of one year's training, one of them was so discouraged that he came to the conclusion that life was not worth living with the kind of handicap he faced.

The other man was so joyful that he went about saying that it was a boon that nature had given people two arms, when he could get along perfectly well with just one!

A positive attitude cannot be taught, it must be caught. Therefore, be careful of the company you keep. If you move in the fellowship of people with positive attitude, their positive vibrations and energy will influence you to develop an optimistic spirit.

Researches at Harvard University have found that graduates who find jobs quickly and get ahead in their job successfully do so because of their positive attitude. In fact the weightage given to the reasons for their success is – 85% for attitude, 15% for their technical skills or other abilities.

That finding must come as an eye opener to many of us. We spend a fortune on educating our children, in giving them foreign degrees and added qualifications, to give them a winning edge. But what do we spend in cultivating a positive attitude! That should indeed set us thinking!

I would also urge you to spend some time in silence everyday. Relax body, mind and spirit by turning thoughts away from your problems and fixing the mind on God. In God is the solution to every problem. When you fix your mind on God and forget your problems, the solutions will come to you spontaneously.

It is so easy to add up our troubles – but it takes some effort to focus on things which we ought to be grateful for. So, even when we are overwhelmed by problems, let us focus our minds on positive things and thank God for all the wonderful things of life – family and friends, sunshine, stars and sky. Let us thank him - for sufferings and disappointments – for they make us evolve spiritually.

Of course, there are bound to be several people who would argue, "How is it possible to say, Thank you God all the time? Just look at the world we live in! It's a terrible place. Consider the times we live in – these are troubled and disturbing times. And we are confronted by problems wherever we turn!"

My answer to them is this: God has faith in us, and He knows that troubles can make us better, stronger human beings.

We must think of solutions, not problems. We must not make problems and grudges the centre of our thinking. We must not blame people or circumstances for our condition.

When people say to themselves again and again, 'I am unhappy', 'I am miserable', 'People are against me', 'Conditions are against me', 'I am overwhelmed by my problems' and so on, they are gripped by a misery of their own making from which there can be no release except through their own effort. They imagine that they are injured beyond repair, and they simply cannot rise above their problems.

Instead, they must affirm to themselves, 'I was born to be happy', 'Happiness is my birthright', 'God created me to be happy'. As their conscious and unconscious thinking changes, conditions and people will also change miraculously. Thought by thought, step by step, as their minds change, the world will also change. And they will find satisfactory solutions to all their problems.

Let me end with the words of best selling author and direct marketing expert, Joseph Sugarman: "Each problem has hidden in it an opportunity so powerful that it literally dwarfs the problem. The greatest success stories were created by people who recognised a problem and turned it into an opportunity."

Focus on Problems vs. Focus on Solutions

When NASA began the launch of astronauts into space, they found out that the pens wouldn't work at zero gravity (ink won't flow down to the writing surface). In order to solve this problem, they hired Andersen Consulting (known as Accenture today). It took them one decade and $12 million. They developed a pen that worked at zero gravity, upside down, underwater, in practically any surface including crystal and in a temperature range from below freezing to over 300 degrees C.

And what do you think the Russians did about the problem?

The Russians used a Pencil !!!

Vadim Kotelnikov

You don't make progress by standing on the sidelines, whimpering and complaining. You make progress by implementing ideas.

Shirley Hufsteddler

Practical Suggestion No.

6

MAKE EVERY OBSTACLE AN OPPORTUNITY

"Why do we have failures at all?" someone asked me. "Why did God not create a world in which there was only success – what a wonderful world it would be!"

But when you come to think of it, it is failures that give a meaning to success. Wherever you have success, there is bound to be failure. The two go together. It is failure that draws out the best that is within us. It is failure that unfolds, unlocks our hidden powers. In the measure in which we face failures in the right spirit, in that measure that the tremendous power that lies locked up within us is unfolded.

It was Roger Von Oech who said, "Most people think of success and failure as opposites, but they are actually products of the same process."

It is only when a person bears failures with faith and courage that he gives the best proof of character that anyone can give. Failure has a place in life. It is very necessary. But even as success is not permanent, failure is not permanent.

We must never ever forget that failures are not final. We fail only when we accept failure as final. We must learn to think of failures as stepping-stones to success, not stopping stones.

There was a young man who had become a chain smoker at the age of 20. When he turned 21, he made a firm resolve to give up smoking for good. "I have smoked hundreds of cigarettes," he said to himself. "Now is the time to give them up."

On the first morning after his resolve it was easy going for him. There was no urge to smoke. The morning passed quickly. But, when he sat down to lunch in the afternoon, he found that his meal was incomplete without a puff. He succumbed to the temptation and had a smoke. This was repeated day after day. Every morning, he made a fresh resolve not to smoke but every afternoon he broke it.

Mark Twain, too, in his writings says: "Smoking is the easiest habit in the world to give up. I ought to know - I have given it up a thousand times!" And so did this young man. But yet he did not give up and accept failure. Everyday he reaffirmed to himself: I have not failed, but I have not yet succeeded. Surely, there will come a time when I will give up smoking. His affirmation was one of latent though not realised success. And the day did come when he gave up smoking. Today even if he moves in the company of chain smokers, he is never tempted.

Never feel that you are a failure. Rather believe that you are on the way to success. Failure occurs only when you accept it as failure. It was Marshall Foch, the great French Army Chief who said "One is never defeated until one accepts it as such."

During the First world war, his country, France, faced many reverses. Everyone thought that France would be defeated but Foch never accepted defeat. He kept on fighting and ultimately attained success.

Someone said to Thomas Alva Edison, the great inventor: "Do you remember Thomas, you failed 24,999 times when you performed those experiments on the storage battery." Edison replied: "No! I have never failed! I had only discovered 24,999 ways in which the storage battery would not work."

Years ago a young man approached Tom Watson, the legendary CEO of IBM, asking for advice as to how he might be more successful. Watson responded simply, "Double your failure rate." The young man walked off and was never heard from again.

As Winston Churchill observed, "People occasionally stumble over the truth, but most pick themselves up and hurry off as if nothing ever happened."

When you stumble on the truth, recognise it! When you stumble on an obstacle, turn it into an opportunity. When you meet with failure, use it as a stepping stone to success.

Marketing experts tell us again and again: Success is the destination. Failure is how you get there. Here is what one of them, Richard Fenton, has to say on the subject: "To achieve significant success in today's world, failure is not just a possibility. It's a requirement. We must see success and failure for what they truly are. They're not opposites, but instead opposite sides of the same coin."

The truth is that fear of failure holds many of us back from achieving our true potential. "The common belief that businesses are more likely to fail than to succeed has led many to forgo the entrepreneurial experience, and the satisfaction and freedom it brings", says a leading business journalist in the U.S. She points out that the rate of failure for small business ventures in the U.S. are quite low; but the perception is that it is rather high; and this makes people afraid to venture into entrepreneurship, and forgoing the possibility of making it big, on their own.

Nothing stops the man who desires to achieve success. The obstacles on his way only strengthen his powers of resolve. Every failure is a course to build his moral muscles.

Soichiro Honda met with countless failures and setbacks over four decades; but he persevered through all obstacles before his Honda Motor Company became one of the largest automobile companies in the world. His inspiring life story has inspired countless entrepreneurs to persevere in the face of adversity and the need for innovation and creativity in periods of failure and loss.

I wonder how many of you have heard of Lance Armstrong. He was an aspiring cyclist, whose ambition was to win the most prestigious cycling event in the world: the famous Tour de France. While he was preparing himself to achieve this cherished goal, he was diagnosed with cancer. It looked as if his cycling career, and maybe even his life, was over. However, he fought back; he fought against his cancer, and he fought on with his desire to achieve his ambition. Would you believe it, he won not one, not two, but as many as seven Tour de France titles. Today he credits his great cycling success to the person he became as a result of having cancer. He says, "Cancer saved my life."

There was a hero who turned obstacles into opportunities!

If you wish to turn failure into success, if you wish to turn every obstacle into an opportunity, the conscious and the subconscious must cooperate with each other. The conscious mind with which we are familiar, the conscious self that thinks, that feels, that takes decisions – this conscious self is a very tiny part of our consciousness. It is like the tip of an iceberg floating above water. The subconscious is much vaster. It is like a larger portion of an iceberg immersed inside the water.

But this subconscious cannot think for itself. It cannot decide what is right and what is wrong. It has no power of decision. If you believe that you cannot achieve something, if you believe that you cannot do something, if you believe that you cannot have something, the subconscious will take up your belief. Its job is only to see that it proves your beliefs. Whatever you believe in, your subconscious will create conditions, so that your beliefs are proved.

The subconscious has tremendous power and uses all that power to reinforce your belief. To achieve success, it is very important that you seek the help of the subconscious. The subconscious is there to receive your orders but you must develop the will to be able to speak to it with magnetic determination. There are times when the subconscious is more receptive to your orders. This is at the time when you are about to slip into sleep and the time when you are about to awaken from sleep. You must have experienced this - that sometimes, after a hectic day you go to sleep with a thought; "I am very tired!" Howsoever long you sleep you will wake up the next morning more often that not, with fatigue. But, if you slip into sleep with the thought, "Surely after this night's rest I am going to wake up feeling refreshed," chances are that you will get up next morning feeling fully refreshed.

Just suppose that there is a fat man who believes that he cannot grow slim, chances are that he will never grow slim. He may go on a crash diet to reduce his weight, but when he is off guard, something will happen, the subconscious will create circumstances so that he is caught in the trap unawares and gains weight.

To turn obstacles into opportunities, you must have strong belief of success, you must paint a picture of yourself succeeding.

If you consciously paint a picture of yourself as a successful person, success will definitely come to you. But if you are convinced that you are a failure – even if you are placed in the best of circumstances, with the best of resources – you will fail! Such is the law. If you think of scarcity, scarcity will befall you. If you imagine abundance, abundance will flow into you.

The universe works like an echo. Whatever thoughts you think, will rebound on you. The picture that we paint of ourselves is assimilated by our subconscious.

The subconscious will immediately try to create those conditions to make your belief come true. But, if on the other hand you strongly believe that you cannot do a particular thing, that it is impossible for you to succeed, the subconscious will create conditions that will lead to your failure. The conscious and the subconscious must cooperate with each other to create success. Success is not produced only by the conscious self. It is done with the help of the subconscious. The subconscious is there to obey you. It is a very obedient servant who takes orders from his master. Its decisions are to be made by you. Its beliefs are to be programmed by you.

There was a servant whose master asked him to bring a few biscuits. He brought the biscuits in his hand. The master scolded him. "You uncouth fellow," he exclaimed. "Don't you know you must bring everything to me on a tray?". The servant said meekly, "Yes master, I will do that. It's a very simple thing after all."

Sometime later the master ordered the servant to bring his shoes. The servant promptly brought them on a plate. Enraged the master shouted, "Stupid fellow, what are you doing?" The bewildered servant replied, "But sir, those were your instructions! I am only obeying your orders."

Our subconscious is like the servant. It cannot think for itself. It cannot decide what is right and what is wrong. It can only obey. The subconscious is like the automatic pilot in an aircraft. If you set the auto-pilot to take the plane eastward, the plane will keep on flying eastward. It is only when you resume manual control that you can change the direction of the plane. This is what the subconscious does too. Therefore, you have to be very careful of the thoughts you think, the affirmations that you make, specially at the time you fall asleep. There are tremendous potentialities open to every one of us. If only we make use of the right affirmations at the right time, we can work wonders!

And positive affirmations pave the way for your success. They make things happen for you. It was Ann Landon who said: "There are only three types of people.

Those who make things happen; those who watch things happen; and those who say, 'What happened?'"

Experts tell us that if we really wish to succeed, we have to accept the fact that we may fail occasionally. Everyone fails at one time or another, but those who know how to react to failures invariably reach success. All we have to do is: Learn from our mistakes; be prepared to face failure, but not dwell on failure constantly; and keep persevering to achieve our goal.

Think about it...

Failure ... Is Only Feedback

Does the thought of failure send a cold shiver down your spine? Failure is the thing most of us spend the greatest amount of energy trying to avoid. What is failure?

In reality, when you strip away all the emotions attached to the word, failure is only feedback. Failure means that we tried a strategy and it did not work. So what should we do? It's simple. We should try something else.

Human beings learn by failure, by understanding what does not work, and by continuing to adjust their strategies until they find out what does work. As young children, we were very familiar with "failure" when we were trying to learn how to walk. How many of us decided one day "Gee, the walking that those adults do looks pretty interesting. I think I'll do it too." And then we got up without a hitch and started walking. Hardly. All of us made countless attempts trying to find out what to do, so we could walk without constantly falling down. As we were learning to walk, we received constant support and praise from the adults in our lives to keep on trying.

Then somewhere down the line we were taught not to take risks, to play it safe, to only do what we knew would bring us success. We have been taught that if we try something and it does not work out as we planned, some terrible event will occur. People will point to us and say, "Look at him. He tried to do _______, but he failed." Oh the shame. So most people will play it safe and never strive to reach their full potential because they might (gasp) fail.

It is true that when we strive to do something that is new for us, we might fail. As a matter of fact, we might fail many times, but only by risking failure will we ever be able to grow. People might also remind us of our failures and tell us they knew it would not work. These people never fail because they never try to accomplish anything with their lives. If you are failing, at least you are doing something.

If you are failing, you are in great company. Most of the super achievers in history failed more often than anyone else. The difference is that they did not let the failure (or the negative comments from others) defeat them. They just continued to modify their strategies until they found what worked. They did not quit. They knew what they wanted and they did not give up until they achieved their goal. When Thomas Edison was attempting to discover the light bulb he was not met with much support from the scientific community. As a matter of fact, they thought he was crazy to try to invent something that was clearly impossible. A young reporter interviewed Edison and asked him, "Mr. Edison, how can you continue to try to invent the light bulb when you have failed over 5,000 times." To which Thomas Edison replied, "Young man, I have not failed 5,000 times. I have successfully discovered 5,000 ways that do not work and I do not need to try them again." This is a great way to interpret failure — as a learning experience.

A powerful way to deal with failure is to ask yourself "What is or could be positive in this situation?" This allows you to obtain some benefit from the experience and then to move on. Very often, we achieve our greatest success right after we have experienced our worst defeat. Nathaniel Hawthorne was a published writer, although he had never achieved remarkable success in the field. Then in 1849, a turning point occurred in his life — he lost his full time job. He dedicated the following year to writing *The Scarlett Letter* which became a classic novel in American Literature. Hawthorne turned a defeat into success.

The bottom line is that we should embrace "failure". Because if we are failing, we are learning; and if we are learning, we are growing. And growing is really what life is all about.

Della Menechella

> I have learned more from my mistakes than from my successes.
>
> **Sir Humphry Davy**

Practical Suggestion No.

7

LEARN TO TAKE RISKS

Let me make this very clear at the outset: when I suggest that you learn to take risks, I do not mean gambling, or hazarding your hard earned money on racing or any such thing! There are numerous definitions of risk available in dictionaries: what I refer to specifically is an action where there is both the probability of making a good profit as well as the possibility of incurring a loss; a chance taken in the hope of a favourable outcome. Today's business environment is full of terms associated with risk, such as: *risk management, risk assessment, credit risk, risk analysis, currency risk, market risk, high risk,* and even *value at risk!* This only goes to prove that the ability to take calculated risks is an essential aspect of successful business management.

"No pains, no gains," says an old fashioned proverb. "Nothing ventured, nothing gained," is another wise saying. It is only because the early *homo sapiens* took calculated risks, that you and I live in the advanced civilisation of the twenty-first century! If your life is absolutely free of failures, chances are that you have not taken risks, and thus lost the chance of learning many valuable lessons in life. Therefore, the management pundits tell us: "The person who risks nothing, does nothing, has nothing, is nothing, and becomes nothing. He may avoid suffering and sorrow, but he simply cannot learn and feel and change and grow and love and live."

Quite apart from success or failure, you learn to face the truth about yourself, when you take risks, with faith in God, and confidence in yourself. You learn to do what you think you cannot do; you learn to do what is hard for you to do; you learn to take the initiative; you learn to take the responsibility for your own actions. As the French humanist Andre Gide tells us, "Man cannot discover new oceans unless he has the courage to lose sight of the shore."

Risk taking must not be confused with thrill-seeking. By this, I mean reckless behaviour, which leads to many sad accidents and avoidable mishaps. Psychologists call this compulsive novelty-seeking behaviour. It is mostly adolescents who indulge in such behaviour to attract attention and enhance their low self-esteem. Ironically enough, it is in the 'developed' countries of the world that such thrill-seeking games abound. Statistics tell us that a disproportionate share of thrill-or sensation-seeking personality types are to be found in the United States, where 'extreme games' such as hang gliding, paragliding and dirt cycling are popular.

The kind of risk taking I am talking about is very different: I refer to situations where we are afraid to venture, because we fear that we may not do well. If we limit ourselves to situations where we are sure of doing well, we will never be able to know what we are capable of achieving. We will simply end up by limiting our own opportunities drastically. Maureen Neihart, a clinical psychologist, tells us that we must appreciate the value of taking risks, and also teach our children about well-planned, systematic risk taking which can help them become high achievers. According to her, there are six steps to systematic risk taking:

1. Understanding the benefits of risk-taking, which include increasing one's confidence, the ability to take on a challenge, increasing a sense of control over one's life, developing skills for coping with anxieties and overcoming fears, and providing practice in important decision making.
2. Initial self-assessment of risk-taking categories: This means the ability to distinguish between intellectual risks, social risks, emotional risks, physical risks, and spiritual risks. Some risks may be easy for us while others will be very difficult.
3. Identifying personal needs: we need to understand and prioritise our own risk levels in different categories. A gifted learner, for example, can take the intellectual risk of appearing for a tough, high-level examination; an athlete might stretch himself to the extreme limit, in order to break a world record; an

ardent lover, might take the emotional risk of declaring his love boldly to his beloved. It all depends on how strongly we feel the need to achieve a particular goal.

4. Choosing the kind of risk that we feel will bring us great satisfaction: this will make the risk more palatable and easy to manage for us.
5. Taking the risk: that is, actually going ahead to take a chance in the interest of our own success.
6. Processing the risk experience: Most of the beneficial changes in people come not as a result of merely *taking* risks, but as a result of processing the risk. The processing that follows risk-taking activities provides for the expression of feelings, and also helps us to clarify our strengths and weaknesses. This can be invaluable for our future growth.

When we are children, we hardly stop to think of risks; we just go ahead and do what we want. But as we grow older, we restrict ourselves. We draw a circle around ourselves and are reluctant to step out of the self-imposed boundaries. We begin to think of the consequences; we fear the repercussions; we even worry about what people might say.

Which is better – to be a reckless doer or a fearful non-doer? The best option is to avoid both extremes. Experts tell us that we must stop thinking of risk as just a do-or-die situation. Instead, we must start thinking of risk as a journey of exploration. It is not about one-shot success or failure; it is about exploring different aspects of our life and personality.

Self-improvement author Brian Kim tells us: "People mistakenly think that if they take a risk and it does not turn out the way they expect it to, then it's all over. The sky will fall, their world will come crashing down, and that they will never bounce back from it. It is precisely because of this 'one shot do or die mentality' that people desist from taking risks. Step back and look at the forest. Don't look at the trees. Risk is not just about looking at one tree. It is about exploring an entire forest."

Dr. Kim adds, significantly: "Columbus did not take a risk. He chose to go on a journey to explore the new world. Entrepreneurs do not take risks. They choose to go on a journey to explore other means of making a living. Companies do not take risks. They choose to explore doing things differently than the norm."

How true! If the great scientists and inventors did not dare to think differently from others, if they had stuck to the beaten tracks and not risked their reputations and their positions to try new things, where would we be today! We would not have airplanes, automobiles or space programmes; we would be without antibiotics and life-saving drugs; nothing ventured, nothing gained!

Doug Sundheim, an executive consultant, had this one question, which he put to each and every one of his clients: *When, at what times in your life, have you felt most alive?* Without exception, each one of them referred to situations in which they stretched themselves well beyond their normal limits to achieve something they had never done before. For instance, when someone with extreme fear of drowning, overcame that fear and learnt to swim. They pushed themselves out of their limited 'comfort zones' to take calculated risks. During these moments, they were not 'afraid of the consequences'; rather, they focused more positively on the great satisfaction that the 'outcome' would provide to them. But when they related these experiences later, they did not emphasise these outcomes; they dwelt with great pleasure on the process of the actual risk-taking.

The counselor concludes: "The gift of risk-taking doesn't lie in what you achieve by risking - it lies in who you *become* as a result of the process. Confident. Engaged. Alive. Furthermore, it isn't something you do once in a while - it's an approach to life. Open. Exploratory. Daring. You know it when you let it slip out of your life. You feel stagnant, lethargic, bored. Today is new. Re-Engage yourself. Learn to take a Risk."

To my mind, learning to take a calculated risk is akin to a leap of faith: it liberates us from fear and helps us engage with life constructively, and accomplish the best we are capable of.

Stepping out of narrow, self-imposed comfort zones; facing challenges; taking tough decisions; innovation and experiments; breaking new ground; building up confidence; accepting our mistakes; learning from our failures; these are the traits of great leaders, and they grow and evolve in stature by taking risks.

Let me close this section with the beautiful lines from a poem by Rabindranath Tagore, "The Song Unsung":

The song that I came to sing remains unsung to this day.
I have spent my days in stringing and in unstringing my instrument.
The time has not come true, the words have not been rightly set;
Only there is the agony of wishing in my heart.
The blossom has not opened; only the wind is sighing by.
I have not seen his face, nor have I listened to his voice;
Only I have heard his gentle footsteps from the road before my house.
The livelong day has passed in spreading his seat on the floor;
But the lamp has not been lit and I cannot ask him into my house.
I live in the hope of meeting with him; but this meeting is not yet.

The problem with stringing and unstringing the instrument over and over again is that sometimes the opportunity to sing our song suddenly and unexpectedly and irretrievably is gone!

We must sing the song which we have come to sing. Each one of us has come to this earth-plane to sing a particular song, a wonderful song that no one else can sing, except us; but we are unable to sing that song because we are not prepared to take the risk. Learn to take risks, so that the beautiful song of your life may be sung to the best of your ability.

Think about it...

Jim Burke became the head of a new products group at Johnson & Johnson. One of his first products was a children's chest rub. It failed miserably and Jim believed he would be fired when he was called into the chairman's office. However, to his surprise, Mr. Johnson asked if he was the one who just cost the company a lot of money and then added. "Well, I want to congratulate you. If you made a mistake, it means you took a risk, and if we don't take risks, we will never grow. That is what business is all about." Years later Jim Burke became the Chairman of Johnson & Johnson.

Our risk preferences are unique to each of us. There is no right or wrong way to be, though some will insist that one way is better than the other and vice versa. In the end, we all have to live with our own decisions, so we should make our own assessments about what makes sense to us.

For those of us that avoid risk, we probably tend to focus more on the potential downside than the potential upside. Yet, just because risk has its downside doesn't mean it should always be avoided at all costs either. Taking risks isn't always a bad thing.

Let's consider what is good about taking risks:

- As we face and overcome smaller fears, we are better able to face bigger and bigger fears.
- After successfully overcoming a fear, we realise that what we once feared is not nearly as scary as we thought it was, so maybe there are other fears that we might be unnecessarily exaggerating, too.
- If we never take the risk, we will have no chance to enjoy its associated rewards.
- Awareness of the potential risk of loss gives us an appreciation for what is around us and within us.
- If things don't go as planned, learning that we can recover from those challenges strengthens us to know we can do it again if need be, making it easier to face other fears.
- Being able to change our focus in order to confront and overcome a fear trains us to be able to control and manage our emotional states in other areas of our lives, too.

Either way, having a healthy respect for risk is a good thing. Regardless of your risk-appetite or need for that adrenaline rush, the consequences of risk, no matter how small, always exist, otherwise it wouldn't be considered a risk.

Weigh the possibilities on both sides of the scale. And, ultimately, don't forget to consider the downside of unnecessarily avoiding calculated risks. How much better could things be if they worked out as good or better than planned, too?

Helen Hoefele

Practical Suggestion No.

8

CULTIVATE THE SPIRIT OF ACCEPTANCE

I would like to pass on to you a *mantra* which is sure to bring you peace, contentment and serenity. It is an expression of your utter and complete faith in the Almighty. It is a prayer which a saint, a holy man of God used to offer again and again. Inscribe it on the tablet of your heart. Repeat it again and again—remember it by day and night, for it is really simple:

Yes Father, Yes Father—Yes and always yes!
Yes Father, Yes Father—Yes and always yes!

There are people who are upset with me because I advocate the philosophy of acceptance. They say to me, that this will make people lazy and lethargic; they will give up all their drive and ambition and simply sink into passive resignation.

I beg to differ with them on this point. I do *not* think people will become lazy and lethargic if they follow the philosophy of acceptance. I believe that true acceptance in the right spirit is a dynamic concept which encourages us to do our very best, to put forth our best efforts to achieve what we desire. But, if we cannot achieve those results, you must accept it as the Will of God, in the knowledge that there must be some good in it. As I always say, there is a meaning of mercy in all the incidents and accidents of life. Therefore, let us accept everything with the *mantra*, "Yes Father, yes, and always, yes!"

There is a meaning of mercy in all that happens to us – for God is all love and all wisdom. He is too loving to punish us. He is too wise to make a mistake. Therefore, if something comes to me that is contrary to my personal will, I must accept it as the Will of God. As Gurudev Sadhu Vaswani taught us, "Every disappointment is His appointment."

An inspector of schools visited our Mira School in Pune. During an interaction with the students, he asked them, "Tell me where is Pune situated?" Many hands shot up, and the children gave the answer in chorus, "In the State of Maharashtra."

"Where is Maharashtra?" the inspector persisted.

"In India," said the children.

"And where is India?"

"In Asia".

"Can you tell me where is Asia?"

"In the world."

"And where is the world?"

A pregnant silence prevailed. But one little girl came out with a sterling answer. "Sir, the world is safe in the Hands of God!"

The world is safe in the Hands of God! Why then should we fret and fume over little disappointments and minor setbacks?

There are so many situations and circumstances in life that are not to our liking. But, how long can we allow ourselves to wallow in sorrow and self-pity? The call of life is *Onward, Forward, Godward*! Men may come and men may go, but life goes on forever! Lives may come to an end, but life on earth must go on!

"Would you know who is the greatest saint in the world?" asks William Law. "It is not he who prays most or fasts most; it is not he who gives most alms or is most eminent for temperance, charity or justice; but it is he who is always thankful to God; who wills everything God wills, who receives everything as an instance of God's goodness and has a heart always ready to praise God for it."

Make this the *mantra* of your life: "Yes Father, yes, and always yes!"

The problems and difficulties that we face in life are sent to us with a definite purpose: we can always derive benefit and wisdom from the most unpleasant experiences. This is why enlightened souls have always expressed gratitude to God in trying times!

It was Dale Carnegie who said, "When we have accepted the worst, we have nothing more to lose. And that automatically means – we have everything to gain."

It is not possible for us, with our limited intelligence, to explain everything that happens in life. Why do I have to struggle, while others succeed effortlessly? Why do I have to face so many disappointments? You can analyse and speculate by all means – but the important thing for you is to accept – take life as it comes and get on with it. It was a wise soul who said: "Acceptance is not submission; it is acknowledgement of the facts of the situation."

When you wish to take on the challenges of life, ask yourself first: what is the worst that can happen to me? The secret of facing life's challenges is to be prepared for the worst – and to hope for the best! Anything in life that we refuse to accept will only impede our progress and constantly irritate us, until we learn to make peace with it.

The Irish dramatist J. M. Synge gave us a beautiful play, called *Riders To The Sea.* It tells us of an old Irish woman, who loses her husband, and all her seven sons one after another. She accepts her loss with fortitude and at the end of the play, when her only remaining son is to be buried, utters the moving prayer: "God, Thou gavest. Thou hast taken away. Blessed be Thy Name!"

By accepting the worst – the loss of her sons – the mother finds release and liberation from sorrow.

Sometime ago, one of the sisters of our Sadhu Vaswani *satsang* came to see me. She was in great emotional distress, and could not keep back her tears as she spoke to me.

Her husband, a kind and devoted man whom she loved dearly, had been posted abroad. She could not accompany him, for his organisation did not permit the families to join employees on such an assignment, for technical reasons.

"I don't want him to leave me and go abroad," she said. "Ask him to give up his job. Or pray that this assignment should be cancelled."

Perhaps my answer might have appeared cruel to her at that time. "I do not pray for this or that to happen," I said to her. "I shall pray instead, that you may grow into an understanding of what God wills for you – and that you may co-operate with His will and let it work uninterrupted, in and through you!"

When her husband left on his assignment, she bade him a tearful farewell. Her face clouded with grief, she said to me, "You did not do anything for me. You could have helped me if you wished to do so!"

I smiled and said to her, "Sister, do not despair! God fulfills Himself in many ways."

After a few months, I had the opportunity to meet her again. She was indeed a transformed creature! Her face was wreathed in smiles. She was as joyous as a child with a new toy.

"Thank you Dada!" she exclaimed. "Now I do know what you meant – there is the Hand of Divine love and wisdom in all that happens. When my husband departed, I was utterly inconsolable. Then, gradually I thought of what you said: if God had willed my dear one to travel to a faraway land, it must also be for my good. And indeed, it has proved to be so. Now that I am alone at home, I have a lot of time to spare. I utilise it to study the *Gita*, the *Guru Granth Sahib* and Sadhu Vaswani's books on the *Sant bani* and the lives of saints – something that I have always wanted to do and never had the *time* to do! I pray and meditate as often as I can. I attend the *satsang* everyday. I sing God's Name and I serve the children of the poor and the lowly. And I feel so happy and blessed!"

The philosophy of wise acceptance had turned her into a radiant soul!

A lady on a long haul transcontinental flight was terrified when the jet hit strong turbulence. Nervously, she asked the flight stewardess, "Are we going to crash?"

"Of course not," the stewardess smiled. "Don't worry. We are all safe in God's Hands."

The woman's eyes widened with shock. "Oh my!" she exclaimed, "Is it that bad?"

"No!" said the stewardess emphatically. "It's that *good*!"

As ordinary mortals, we have so many imperfections, defects, errors, weaknesses and insufficiencies. We are often overcome by doubt and insecurities. It becomes essential that we all learn to put ourselves in God's hands and allow ourselves to be guided by His Divine Wisdom.

It was a hot day. Naseeruddin Hodja sat under a walnut tree, looking at his pumpkin vines.

He said to himself, "God is indeed foolish! Here He puts the heavy, large pumpkin on this delicate creeper which can only lie on the ground. And He puts these tiny walnuts on a big tree whose branches can easily hold the weight of a man! Now, if I were God, I'm sure I can do better than that!"

Just then a gust of wind blew; it dislodged a walnut which fell on the head of Hodja.

"Ouch!" exclaimed Hodja, rubbing his head, a sadder and wiser man. "God is right after all! Now, if it had been a pumpkin up there, instead of a tiny walnut, what would have become of me! Never again will I try to plan the world for God – but I shall thank God that He has planned the world so well!

In God's Providence, everything comes to pass at the right time.

The sun rises at the right time: the stars appear at the right time: the seasons change at the right time.

Put forth the best that you are capable of. Leave the results in the safe hands of the Lord. He will never fail you!

Leave it to God – and He will take care of everything!

Many people tell me: we work so hard, we work so strenuously, and yet we achieve nothing. We work for the good of the community, society, nation and humanity. We sacrifice our health, wealth, rest and leisure. Yet, our work produces no effect: it gives us no satisfaction. The world speeds on, from danger to destruction, and our life is reduced to never ending cycle of work, tension and frustration!

The reason for this is that our work is not in tune with the Divine Will. Our work is tainted with the self – desire for prominence, desire for recognition, or even thought of reward in the life beyond. We have not relinquished control to God!

Sadhu Vaswani used to tell us, "God upsets our plans to set up His own. And His plans are always perfect."

If I have the faith that whatever has happened to me is according to the plan of the Highest, that there is some hidden good in it for me, I will not be upset!

Yes Father—Yes and always Yes!

Acceptance in the spirit of gratitude unlocks the fullness in our lives. It can turn despair into faith, strife into harmony, chaos into order, and confusion into clear understanding. It restores peace into our hearts and helps us to look forward to the morrow in the faith that God is always with us!

It is not enough to speak of gratitude or enact deeds of gratitude—we must *live* gratitude by practising acceptance of God's Will in all conditions, in all incidents and accidents of life.

When things are not going as we wish, we tend to develop 'tunnel vision'—that is, focus on the dark, negative side of life. However, we will do well to remember that it is always darkest before dawn and trial and adversity can be powerful agents of change that help us grow, evolve to become better human beings, and eventually make a success of our lives.

There are several things in our lives about which we are not happy. Our 'wish list' for something different, something more, something other than what we possess extends to several aspects of our daily life.

A psychiatrist has described depression as "anger turned inward." We are angry with so many things and so many people; we are discontented with the way we live our lives—and we are angry with ourselves.

If we persist with depression, discontent and anger, it will not be long before we start blaming God for all the ills that beset us!

- God could have made me taller, slimmer, more beautiful.
- God could have given me more money, a richer husband, a more understanding wife, kinder parents, better friends.
- God could have made my children more intelligent, more accomplished, more obedient, more appreciative...

The list is endless!

So the blame shifts to God! Are we not accusing Him of being unfair, unjust, and unkind when we perceive our life to be all wrong? In the end it all turns out to be His fault!

Patience and acceptance are difficult to cultivate. Without them, there can be no inner development, no spiritual growth.

That is not at all! When we lack the wisdom to accept God's Will, we cause ourselves a lot of unnecessary grief; grief that arises because reality differs from our wishes and our plans.

It was a wise soul who prayed, "Lord give me the strength to change the things I can change, patience to accept the things I cannot change, and wisdom to know the difference."

Wisdom consists in accepting what you cannot change. What cannot be cured must be endured. This is not passive resignation or pessimistic self-denial. It is the way of wisdom which leads to peace.

We need to grow in the spirit of acceptance, for life is full of unexpected events. A dear one is snatched away from us suddenly. Initially, we are devastated; we weep, we shed bitter tears; we refuse to eat, we cannot sleep.

That is but natural, you might say. But how long can you go on? Will weeping, fasting and vigil bring back your loved one to life?

And then again, aren't we all mortal? Can we determine the length and duration of our own life—or anyone else's life?

Wisdom consists in accepting God's Will—not with despair or resignation, but in peace and faith, knowing that our journey through life has been perfectly planned by Infinite love and Infinite wisdom. There can be no mistake in God's Plan for us!

Again and again, we try to run away from difficult situations; again and again we rebel, react with anger and bitterness. How can we ever be at peace?

The answer is simple: Grow in the spirit of surrender to God; develop the spirit of acceptance. "Not my will, but Thy Will be done, O Lord!" this must be the constant utterance on your lips.

To seek refuge is to trust the Lord—fully, completely, entirely. It is to know that He is the one Light that we need in the darkest hours of our life. He is the all-loving One whose ears are ever attentive to the prayers of His wayward children. He is the all-knowing One who does the very best for us. With Him, all things are possible: and if, He chooses *not* to do certain things for us which we want Him to do, it is not because He cannot do them, but because He knows better—He knows we require something else for our own good.

So it is that he who has taken refuge in the Lord is ever at peace. "Not my will, but Thy Will be done, O Lord," he prays. Whatever happens, "I accept! I accept! I accept!" is his *mantra*. "Yes Father, Yes and always Yes!" is his response to all incidents and all accidents of life. Nothing—no accident, no loss, no tragedy—can disturb his equanimity.

For your reflection...

Sometimes your biggest weakness can become your biggest strength. Take, for example, the story of this 10-year-old boy who decided to study judo despite the fact that he had lost his left arm in a devastating car accident.

An old Japanese judo master agreed to take him on as his pupil. The boy was earnest and sincere, and came for his lessons everyday. But he couldn't understand one thing: why, after three months of training, the master had taught him only one move.

"Sensei," the boy said to his master one day, "Shouldn't I be learning a few more moves?"

"This is the not just the only move you know, but this is the only move you'll ever need to know," the sensei replied.

The boy couldn't quite understand what this meant; but he had great faith in his teacher; so he accepted the teacher's word and kept on training with him.

Several months later, the sensei took the boy to his first tournament. Surprising himself, the boy easily won his first two matches, using the one move that he had been taught. The third match proved to be a little more difficult, but after some time, his opponent became impatient and charged; the boy deftly used his one move to win the match. Still amazed by his success, the boy was now in the finals.

This time, his opponent was bigger, stronger, and more experienced. For a while, the boy appeared to be overmatched. Concerned that the boy might get hurt, the referee called a time-out. He was about to stop the match when the sensei intervened.

"No," the sensei insisted, "Let him continue."

Soon after the match resumed, his opponent made a critical mistake: he dropped his guard. Instantly, the boy used his one move to pin him. The boy had won the match and the tournament. He was the champion!

On the way home, the boy and the sensei reviewed every move in each and every match. Then the boy summoned the courage to ask what was really on his mind.

"Sensei, how did I win the tournament with only one move?"

"You won for two reasons," the sensei answered. "First, you've almost mastered one of the most difficult throws in all of judo, for that was the one move I taught you. Second, the only known defense for that move is for your opponent to grab your left arm..."

The boy's biggest weakness had become his biggest strength! And he had capitalised on his faith to turn his weakness into his advantage.

Conclusion

What Is Impossible for Man is Possible for God!

I am sure all of you have heard of Napoleon Hill, the inspirational writer: he tells us in his book, *Think and Grow Rich*, "One of the main weaknesses of mankind is the average man's familiarity with the word 'impossible.' He knows all the rules which will not work. He knows all the things which cannot be done."

Napoleon Hill has been hailed as the "Founder of The Science of Success" by millions of readers whom he has inspired with his motivational books. His motto was: "Whatever your mind can conceive and believe it can achieve."

Napoleon Hill was born into poverty in 1883 in a one-room cabin on the Pound River in Wise County, Virginia. At the age of ten he lost his mother, and grew up under the care of a stepmother. He began writing at the age of thirteen as a "mountain reporter" for small town newspapers; this helped him to pay part of his fees at law school. To finance his own education, he took up an assignment to write a series of success stories of famous men, and his big break came when he was asked to interview steel-magnate Andrew Carnegie. Mr. Carnegie commissioned Hill to interview over 500 millionaires to find a success formula that could be used by the average person. (We are told that Carnegie did not pay him any money at first; only letters of introduction were provided to him!) The distinguished men whom he interviewed reads like the Who's Who of the great American Dream: Thomas Edison, Alexander Graham Bell, Henry Ford, Elmer Gates, Charles M. Schwab, Theodore Roosevelt, William Wrigley Jr., John Wanamaker, William Jennings Bryan, George Eastman, Woodrow Wilson, William H. Taft, John D. Rockefeller, F. W. Woolworth, Jennings Randolph, among others.

It took Hill over 20 years to produce his book, a classic in the Personal Development field called *Think and Grow Rich*. This book has sold over 7 million copies worldwide and has helped thousands achieve success.

Coming from an underprivileged background, fighting against great disadvantages and pressures, Napoleon Hill became a source of inspiration to many people who aspired to succeed in their lives. He passed away in November 1970 after a long and successful career writing, teaching, and lecturing about the principles of success. His work stands as a monument to individual achievement and is the cornerstone of modern motivation .

What exactly is the secret of achievement offered to readers of *Think and Grow Rich*? To tell you the truth, it is not really offered to us directly. It is not even explicitly identified. Hill felt that discovering the secret for themselves would provide readers with the most benefit. Therefore he presented the idea, "Define a Major Purpose" as a challenge to his readers in order to make them ask themselves, "In what do I truly believe?" For according to him, 98% of people had no firm beliefs, and this alone put true success firmly out of their reach.

Let me ask you the same question: in what do you truly believe?

I had met a young college student some time ago. "Life is like a maze, a riddle," he complained. "I feel confused, confounded. I see no way out of the perplexities and problems which baffle me again and again. I feel like a child who has lost his way in a huge fair. What do you think I should do?"

I said to him, "Was there a time in your life when you were really not confused or worried?"

"Yes," he laughed bitterly. "It was probably when I was one-and-a-half years old. And I hardly remember it now, but I know I had a happy, carefree childhood!"

"Exactly," I said to him. "If I become a child, I do not have to worry. The child trusts its mother and knows that the mother will always keep it safe from harm."

"You too, can become a child," I continued. "For that matter, so can all of us. All we need to do is hand ourselves over to the Lord – and He will take care of everything."

As we all know, the child is singularly free from worries and cares, for it knows, beyond a shadow of doubt, that the mother is there to provide for all its needs. As for the mother, she anticipates the needs of her children and provides for them well in advance. We who think we are independent only create for ourselves a situation in which we take on our burdens and struggle with them, suffering from accumulated stress and tension. We need to grow in the realization that we have nothing to fear, when our Divine Mother is near. With God, all things are possible!

I encourage my friends to look upon God as their Mother. Who are we to define and limit God to the masculine form? God is all things to all of us. When we think of God as our Mother, we free ourselves from the pressure and insecurity of imagining that God is someone to fear and keep our distance from. When a child has fallen into a ditch and made himself filthy, he runs to his mother and tells her, "Ma, I've become filthy. Wash me and clean me!" There is no hesitation, no doubt in is mind that his mother will set everything right for him. This is how we must all feel about God.

"The strong alone can shoulder the burden!" sings a well-beloved poet of Sind. Our problem is that we do not realize our strength as children of God. We try to lift heavy loads on our weak shoulders, when we can so easily entrust them to One for whom all the burden of all the universe is as a feather's weight. Weighed down by burdens which we cannot and need not carry, we move through life, travailing and groaning in needless agony and pain. All we need to do is go within and make contact with the Mother Divine, and cast our cares at Her Lotus feet. Then, we may well move along the pathways of life, singing as we go!

If we wish to make the impossible possible, let us know God, and develop contact with Him! All around us is the sorry spectacle of restless men rushing in headlong speed, moving mechanically from one task to another, achieving nothing, not knowing where they are going. To such people, I appeal: Learn to be still! Place your trust in God – with whom all things are possible!

To be still is not to be lazy or indolent. To be still is to be relaxed, restful, in the awareness that you are safe in God's hands. Do not take on too much. Do not rush through your daily tasks. Move calmly, slowly, quietly from one duty to another, pausing again and again, for a brief while, to pray and rest at the Mother's feet. Tell her, "This work, O Mother Beloved, is Thine! May I be but an instrument of Thy Will Divine!"

This aspiration has the power to transform even the most mundane work into a sacrament. This aspiration keeps the contact alive and makes our work a source of blessing and inspiration to all who cross our path. We will find too, that our efforts are crowned by success, and our lives will become joyous.

You must remember, it is not the amount of work we do that matters, but the *way* we do it. It is not *what* we do, but *how* we do it that determines our success. There are many people who toil and drudge and slave, day after day, month after month, year after year: their work brings them no joy; it is as a shadow on the wall. It vanishes without leaving a trace. True work, abiding work, the work that may transform lives, is that which flows out of the centre of the heart, the centre of harmony and happiness, peace and joy. Let God occupy this centre, and you are sure to find your work and life transformed.

Believe that with God, all things are possible! Many doctors have assured us that they have seen men, after all therapy had failed, lifted out of affliction and disease by the serene effect of faith. Faith, indeed, seems to overcome even the so-called 'laws of nature'. And the occasions on which prayer has dramatically done this have been termed 'miracles.'

Are you one of those disgruntled people who feel that your life has had no miracles? Let me tell you, a constant, quieter miracle is taking place every day, every hour, every minute in the lives of men who have placed their trust in the Lord, and find His sustaining power flowing into their daily lives.

Trust in the Lord! In faith, you achieve harmony of body, mind and spirit which gives unshakeable strength to your weakest efforts. Did not Jesus say, "Ask and it shall be given to you?" True, prayer cannot bring the dead back to life, or wipe away pain and suffering. But prayer, like radium, is a source of luminous energy that can light up our lives.

As human beings, we seek to augment our finite energy by linking ourselves to God, who is the source of infinite energy. His power is inexhaustible, and He is ready to give some of it to us so that we may do what we have to do. Just by asking for His help, our deficiencies are set right and we are restored, rejuvenated and strengthened. With Him, all things are possible!

By myself, I can do nothing: that is the very first principle of spiritual life. The second principle is – He that is within you is greater than he that is outside. To us, external forces appear to be strong and powerful. But they are nothing compared to that which is within you – the Lord, who is seated in the throne of your heart, for whom everything is possible.

Significant are the words of the great German mystic, Meister Eckhart: "Where creature stops, there God begins. All God wants of thee is to go out of thyself in respect of thy creatureliness and let God be the God-in-thee."

Let God take over our lives, for He makes the impossible possible!

There was a senior executive who was sent to attend a workshop on motivation and positive thinking. Every participant was given course material and inspirational CDs to take home. The executive would play the CDs aloud every evening, to reinforce the ideas he had picked up at the workshop. His little daughter would sit with him and listen to the CDs along with her father. The father never imagined that his little girl really understood what all those positive thinkers were saying.

One day, the girl returned from school waving her latest test results. She had got nine out of ten in her test – the highest in class. Where had she lost that one mark? Asked to give the meaning of the word "impossible" her answer was: "There is no such word. Nothing is impossible!"

How I wish all of us, adults, would grasp the idea of our unlimited potential! All of us must understand that nothing is impossible, when we have God on our side.